NORTH AMERICAN
BIRD
IDENTIFIER

NORTH AMERICAN
BIRD
IDENTIFIER

RICK IMES

MALLARD PRESS

MALLARD PRESS

An Imprint of BDD Promotional Book Company, Inc.
566 Fifth Avenue
New York, N.Y. 10103

'Mallard Press and its accompanying design and logo are trademarks of BDD Promotional Book Company, Inc.'

Copyright 1991 Quintet Publishing Limited

First published in the United States of America in 1991 by the Mallard Press

ISBN 0–7924–5512–6

This book was designed and produced by
Quintet Publishing Limited
6 Blundell Street
London N7 9BH

Creative Director: Terry Jeavons
Designer: Chris Dymond
Illustrator: Danny McBride
Project Editor: Lindsay Porter
Editor: Amanda O'Neil
Picture Research: Rick Imes

Typeset in Great Britain by
Central Southern Typesetters, Eastbourne
Manufactured in Hong Kong by
Regent Publishing Services Limited
Printed in Hong Kong by Leefung-Asco Printers Limited

Picture Credits

Contents

What Are Birds?

Loons, such as this common loon, are considered by ornithologists to be North America's most primitive bird species.

Origins

Such marvelously different creatures are birds that anyone with even a passing interest in them must eventually wonder about their origins. Superficially, they bear little resemblance to most other animals, but the scales on their beaks and legs and their habit of laying eggs indicates a relationship with reptiles. In fact, many scientists now believe that dinosaurs never became completely extinct, and that their descendants now live among us as – birds!

There is good evidence supporting this assertion. Paleontologists have established that many dinosaur species, once considered to have been cold-blooded reptiles, were actually warm-blooded, as are birds. The first direct link with dinosaurs was established in 1861, when the first fossil of a species known as *Archaeopteryx lithographica* was unearthed from a limestone quarry in Bavaria. Its feathers were nearly identical to those of modern birds, and it possessed a pelvis, shoulders, and legs similar to today's birds. The rest of its skeleton, however, was decidedly reptilian, with a dinosaur-like skull, teeth, clawed fingers, abdominal ribs, and a long bony tail. *Archaeopteryx*, in turn, is believed to have evolved, along with dinosaurs, from two-legged, lizard-like reptiles living in the Jurassic Period, approximately 160 million years ago.

Classification

Scientists around the world categorize organisms by means of a classification hierarchy, a series of divisions arranged from general to detailed relationships. Each is a collective unit composed of one or more groups from the next more specific level. In order of increasing specificity they are: kingdom, phylum, class, order, family, genus, and species. A kingdom is composed of a group of closely related phyla, each of which is a group of associated classes, and so on.

The genus and species are combined to form the scientific name of the organism, which is always underlined or italicized. The generic name is always capitalized, while the specific name never is, and when writing about several members of the same genus, the generic name may, after its first mention, be abbreviated (F. *peregrinus* for *Falco peregrinus*, for example). This practice, known as the system of binomial nomenclature, was introduced in 1753 by Swedish

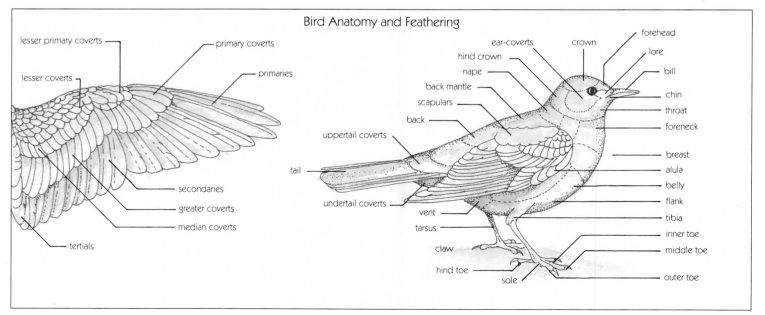

Bird Anatomy and Feathering

lesser primary coverts
primary coverts
lesser coverts
primaries
secondaries
greater coverts
median coverts
tertials

forehead
ear-coverts
crown
lore
hind crown
bill
nape
back mantle
chin
scapulars
throat
back
foreneck
uppertail coverts
breast
tail
alula
belly
undertail coverts
flank
vent
tibia
tarsus
inner toe
claw
middle toe
hind toe
outer toe
sole

Major Groups of Common North American Birds

Order Gaviiformes—**loons**

Order Podicipediformes—**grebes**

Order Pelecaniformes—**pelicans, cormorants, anhinga, gannet**

Order Anseriformes—**swans, geese, ducks, mergansers**

Order Falconiformes—**vultures, hawks, eagles, osprey, falcons**

Order Galliformes—**turkeys, grouse, pheasants, quail, ptarmigan**

Order Ciconiiformes—**herons, bitterns, storks, ibises**

Order Gruiformes—**cranes, rails, gallinules, coot**

Order Charadriiformes—**gulls, terns, sandpipers, turnstones, plovers, stilts, avocets, phalaropes, woodcock, snipe, skimmers**

Order Columbiformes—**doves, pigeons**

Order Cuculiformes—**cuckoos, roadrunner**

Order Stigiformes—**owls**

Order Caprimulgiformes—**goatsuckers**

Order Apodiformes—**swifts, hummingbirds**

Order Coraciiformes—**kingfishers**

Order Piciformes—**woodpeckers**

Order Passeriformes—**flycatchers, larks, swallows, jays, magpie, crows, chickadees, titmice, nuthatches, creepers, wrens, mockingbirds, thrashers, thrushes, solitaire, bluebirds, gnatcatchers, kinglets, waxwings, starlings, vireos, warblers, finches, blackbirds, orioles, tanagers, grosbeaks, sparrows, longspurs**

naturalist Carolus Linnaeus, replacing the cumbersome method of a generic name followed by a series of descriptive phrases. Using the scientific name allows scientists to know exactly which organism they are discussing. Common names are much less precise, as one organism may have several common names or may share the same common name with other species.

Birds are, obviously, members of the Animal Kingdom. Their possession of a backbone places them in the most advanced group of animals, the Phylum Chordata. All birds compose the Class Aves, which is further divided into orders, families, genera, and species. The entire classification of the American robin, for example, is Kingdom Animalia (animals), Phylum Chordata (animals with backbones), Class Aves (birds), Order Passeriformes (perching birds), Family Turdidae (thrushes, solitaires, and bluebirds), Species *Turdus migratorius*.

Feathers & The Miracle of Flight

Feathers define birds. All birds have feathers, but no other creatures possess them. In the earliest stages, the development of a bird's feathers very closely resembles that of a reptile's scales, further suggesting a relationship between the two groups. It is likely that the first feathers actually evolved as modified scales that functioned as fluffy, heat-conserving insulation. They later evolved into more complex structures with specialized functions. Mature feathers contain no living cells and receive nothing but physical support from the body.

There are six feather types. A **vaned feather**, the most familiar type, is composed of a central shaft, or rachis, and a vane consisting of two opposite webs of interlocking barbs which form the flexible, relatively flat plane essential to flight. Adjacent barbs are held together in parallel by overlapping barbules with microscopic hooks and flanges. Should the barbs become separated, they can be easily restored in zipper-like fashion by the preening action of a bird's bill. Vaned feathers which form the outermost covering of a bird's body and provide its streamlined shape are called contour feathers, while those extending beyond the body and making flight possible are known as flight feathers. The outermost flight feathers on a wing are called primaries, while the innermost are the secondaries.

Down feathers are fluffy because their barbules are arranged somewhat randomly and have no hooks. Hidden under the contour feathers of mature birds, they are short and abundant, functioning mainly as insulation. **Semiplume feathers** have barbs arranged in two opposite rows, just as in vaned feathers, but their barbules also lack hooks, making them downy in nature. These provide flexibility for the movement

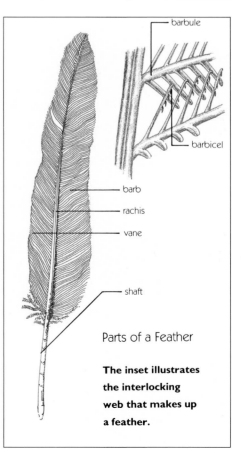

barbule

barbicel

barb

rachis

vane

shaft

Parts of a Feather

The inset illustrates the interlocking web that makes up a feather.

Types of feather: 1) filoplume; 2) pheasant vane with aftershaft; 3) vane or contour; 4) down; 5) semiplume.

of the contour feathers under which they are found, as well as insulation and buoyancy, especially in water birds. Whip-like **filoplume feathers** are closely associated with flight feathers. The abundance of nerve endings in the follicles at the base of filoplumes provide precise control over the movement of flight feathers. **Bristles**, modified contour feathers without vanes, may form protective eyelashes or dust filters in nostrils. They may also form a touch-sensitive net around the mouths of birds that catch insects on the wing. **Powder down feathers** grow continuously and never molt. Instead, their tips constantly disintegrate into a fine, water-resistant powder. Spread by preening or fluffing the feathers, this powder waterproofs and preserves the feathers and lends a metallic sheen to the plumage of some species.

Overall, we see that the major functions of feathers are flight, protection, and, in water birds, buoyancy. Feathers provide a cushioning shield that protects the body against physical damage, rain, and solar radiation. Birds have great control over their internal body temperature, regulating it by fluffing or sleeking their insulating layer of feathers as necessary.

Buoyancy is provided by the oiled, rough-textured contour feathers of aquatic birds that form a water-repellent barrier that also traps air in the downy layer of feathers beneath them. A preen gland on the rump of most birds provides the oil that conditions and waterproofs feathers, leg scales, bills, and talons. This oil is applied lightly to the bird's plumage through the act of preening, or grooming, with the bill.

Feathers, being very complex structures, require much more care than either skin, scales, or hair, and preening therefore occupies a good bit of a bird's time. Birds in drier regions frequently take dust baths, while those of more humid climates take either dust or water baths. Baths are followed by preening, which restores powder down or oil to the feathers and repairs separated vanes. Bathing, preening, and

scratching with claws relieve itching, remove parasites, and clean and restore the feathers.

Birds routinely undergo the process of molting. Old feathers loosen and are pushed out of their follicles by new feathers growing beneath them. While the main purpose of molting is to replace worn feathers, some species undergo a partial molt just before breeding season to expose brilliant courtship plumage. Adults usually molt once every year, often right after the breeding

season. In a remarkable adaptation, this energy-consuming event conveniently occurs between the breeding season and fall migration, two physically-demanding periods, and coincides with a season of abundant food and warm temperatures. In most birds, the molting pattern is such that flight feathers are shed symmetrically, a few at a time, so as not to interfere with flight. Most perching birds molt their primaries progressively from the innermost to the outermost on each wing. However, many large-bodied water birds, including ducks, geese, swans, and loons, fly poorly or not at all with only one or two pairs of primaries missing. Instead, they seek a sheltered retreat and molt all of their primaries simultaneously, replacing them during a short but flightless period.

Flight feathers, visible on the wings of these snow geese as they land, differ in structure and function from other types of feathers.

Many of the aerodynamic features of modern aircraft were copied from birds. Their streamlined shapes and smooth contours produce minimal resistance to air currents, and the airflow over their curved wing profiles produces lift. The primaries, or large outer wing feathers, have a most efficient design. The barbs on the leading edge of the feather are short and stout for strength. Those on the primary's trailing edge are longer and more flexible, curling up on the downstroke and down on the upstroke in a motion that provides both lift and forward thrust. It has been found that the primaries of the stronger fliers have firmer vanes than those of weaker fliers due to the presence of stronger, longer hooks on their barbules. Tail feathers serve mainly as a rudder and brake, although soaring birds will often spread their tails wide to take advantage of the extra lift that this affords.

We cannot discuss feathers without mentioning color. As a group, birds rival insects and tropical fish as the world's most colorful creatures, and their brilliant hues serve several functions. Colors and patterns aid in species recognition, allowing territorial males to recognize and drive away rivals during the breeding season, helping to attract a mate, and keeping gregarious birds together while migrating or establishing a nesting colony. Because of the dangers posed by predators, however, conspicuous, colorful males usually must refrain from visiting the nest site often, and many molt to a drab color after the breeding season for personal safety. Colors and patterns are highly variable in the bird world, so much so that often a single feather is sufficient to identify the species it belongs to.

Behavior

Nearly all behavior in the animal kingdom has as its ultimate objective the survival of an individual's genes, which occurs only with successful reproduction and the survival of offspring to sexual maturity. Genes are selfish; they care nothing for the rest of

Among birds, monogamy often means pairing only for the breeding season. This is especially true among small migratory birds, like Kentucky warblers, which winter in Central and South America.

their species, only that their host survives and reproduces as efficiently as possible, passing along the maximum number of its genes via offspring.

To this end, genes direct an animal's behavior. Animals programmed by their genes to act (or react) in ways that enhance their ability to survive, to attract mates, to dominate rivals, etc., will propagate more, passing along more of the very genes that produced the advantageous behavior. Those who are less able to attract mates and defend them against rivals, avoid predators, hold territories, or feed themselves will pass on fewer genes. The inefficient genes are eventually overwhelmed by a greater number of superior genes and disappear from the gene pool. Those animals who behavior threatens their survival may not live long enough to reproduce at all, thus eliminating defective genes from the species' gene pool.

This is the very essence of the process of natural selection, or "survival of the fittest." It explains how organisms are able to evolve from primitive to more advanced life forms. In the light of this, one could convincingly argue that we are all simply vehicles motivated by our genes to achieve their objectives.

Birds exhibit some of the most complex and intriguing behavior in the animal kingdom. Volumes have been written on the subject, of a magnitude we could not hope

to approach in these pages. Instead, we shall draw your attention to the basic types of behavior so that you can do your own research and make your own observations.

CALLS AND SONGS – Bird songs increase in complexity, volume, and vitality with the approach of the breeding season, reaching their peak at the time of courtship and nesting. From this we can deduce that they originated in conjunction with reproduction. Indeed, they continue to function primarily as an aid to reproduction, specifically in courtship and territoriality. The urge to sing is triggered by hormonal changes in the bird, which in turn become elevated, in the middle and northern latitudes, mainly in response to the increasing length of the daylight period in the spring.

With practice, most birds can be identified by song alone. This is especially helpful with the many species of woodland birds that spend the majority of their time high in the forest canopy, obscured by foliage. Since it is nearly impossible to describe bird songs accurately in print, they are not covered in the Species Sampler. The best way to learn bird songs is to listen to one of the excellent recordings on the market which identify each song by species. Rather than trying to memorize all bird songs at once, go out in the field and listen to one or more songs, then try to locate them on your recording.

Singing is directed at other members of the same species, so it is natural that, with few exceptions, songs are unique to a particular species. In most, but not all, cases, singing ability is more highly developed in males than in females, reflecting the differing roles of the sexes. Songs can identify an individual, announce its sex, induce another bird to reveal its sex, lure a mate, rebuff a rival, indicate rank in the local "pecking order", stake a claim to territory, and perform a number of other functions.

The importance of song to a particular species is indicated by the amount of time and energy the bird devotes to it. This, too, will vary under differing circumstances. The males of a very territorial species, such as the indigo bunting, will sing much more often when the area is saturated with rival males than he would if his territory were fairly isolated from others of the same species.

Some birds make only the most rudimentary sounds that could not be described as song by any stretch of the imagination. You can expect the biology of such a species to be quite different from one that spends a large percentage of its waking hours during the breeding season in song. The more primitive birds, colonial nesters, and birds that feed on the open sea or on the wing have no need to select and defend large territories, hence the lesser importance of song in their lives.

Calls are shorter, simpler, and generally less musical than songs. They also serve some very different purposes. There are alarm calls that warn of danger, summoning calls used by parents to rally their young, begging calls imploring parents to feed nestlings, cohesive calls that hold a flock together when visibility is poor, spacing calls that prevent midair collisions among tight-flying flocks, signature calls that identify species and individuals, calls that convey information about food sources, enemies, etc., and several others. Sometimes calls and songs are used to release nervous energy or to indicate the emotional state of the bird.

COURTSHIP – Song is but one part of the very ritualized courtship behavior in birds. Courtship is highly individualized among the various species, in part to ensure recognition and to prevent time and energy from being wasted on courting another of the same sex or even of a different species. In species whose sexes are externally similar, both sexes often participate equally in courtship, so the birds must first establish who's who through specific methods. The classic example of this is the penguin. When a male is seeking a mate, he places a pebble at the feet of another bird. If he mistakenly makes the offering to another male, the indignant recipient is likely to start a fight. An unreceptive female will ignore the gift, but if she is ready for courtship, she signals this and the pair initiates their various displays.

Courtship enables a male, through the vigor and skill of his displays, to advertise his fitness as a mate to available females. Since in most cases it is the female who selects the male, a female's response is equally critical, telling the male whether or not his advances have been accepted. Reciprocal courtship responses strengthen their bond, keeping the pair together.

Calls convey specific messages. The calls of nestlings trigger feeding response from their parents.

Through their responses, the pair also synchronize their reproductive efforts, delaying the actual process of mating until the proper time, again ensuring a successful mating and avoiding wasted time and energy.

In addition to song, courtship rituals may include dances, aerial displays, posturing, sound production other than voice, the offering of gifts or food, and the exhibition of breeding plumage and other sexual characteristics. Such rituals not only serve to attract a mate and establish a pair bond, but also to warn away competing members of the same species.

TERRITORIALITY – Basically, territoriality means claiming a certain piece of real estate to the exclusion of all others of the same species, with the exception of mates and immediate offspring. Not all birds are territorial, but among those that are, there are several reasons why they should expend the considerable time and energy necessary to acquire and defend a territory.

The ability to claim and successfully defend a choice territory is a good indication of a male's fitness as a mate and of the superiority of his genes. Thus, the quality of a male's empire may very well determine the calibre of the mate he succeeds in attracting. An individual of a territorial species who is unable to assert himself over a decent territory may very well fail to mate that season.

Another major reason is to secure a suitable nest site. Nest location alone can determine the success or failure of a breeding pair's reproductive efforts. In the eyes of a bird, a good nest site may be one well-hidden from predators, providing good support, within a reasonable distance of reliable food and water supplies, and safe from floods, high winds, and most other natural catastrophes. Undoubtedly there are other factors whose importance is known only to the birds themselves.

Perhaps nest sites are fairly plentiful, but the species has a specialized diet. In this case, the bird nests on the territory but the primary reason for staking it out is to secure enough food for the breeding pair and their brood or broods by limiting the competition from others of their species. The size of this territory may vary greatly, depending upon the density of food and the appetites of the birds.

Some species claim a feeding territory but nest elsewhere. This occurs among species that feed in one habitat but prefer to nest in another. Rufous hummingbirds will stake out their own patch of wildflowers in a meadow but build their nest in a tree some distance away. While on the territory, the hummingbirds feed while patrolling an ever-decreasing perimeter. In this way, any intruders would have to challenge the bird's defenses before reaching the nectar-rich flowers in the interior. Great blue herons and great egrets likewise defend a feeding territory but nest colonially in rookeries, sometimes a fair distance away.

For some birds, especially colonial species, the territory often consists only of a nest site because their food source is either plentiful, unpredictable, widely distributed, or otherwise impractical to defend. Such species typically feed in the ocean or other large bodies of water, or in the air. Their territories are usually quite small, often just large enough to accommodate the nest. Under these conditions, the quality of the territory may depend upon its location within the colony. If the nest sites in the interior of the colony are the most secure from predators, it is likely that those sites will be held by the dominant members of the colony.

NESTING – Like everything else in the world of birds, their nesting practices vary greatly. Nest range in size from the thimble-like constructions of hummingbirds to those of bald eagles which, after many years of use, may exceed 8 feet in diameter and 12 feet in depth, and weigh 2 tons or more.

The complexity of a nest also differs from one species to another. While the grand

Osprey nests, used year after year, can grow into massive, complex structures of woven sticks. They are nearly always found over or near water, the food source for the osprey, which eats fish exclusively.

prize for sophistication has to go to the northern oriole and its intricately woven, pendulous nest, others like the turkey vulture make do with no structure at all, simply laying their eggs on the ledge of a cliff. The brown-headed cowbird goes one up on the vultures. It is a brood parasite, meaning that it lays its eggs in other birds' nests, leaving the foster parents to raise the aggressive chick.

In most species, the female is the major architect and builder of the nest, although the male may help with building or collecting materials. The construction materials used depends upon the species, but some of the more common ones are grass, plant fibers, hair, twigs, mud, string, pine needles, and moss. These components camouflage the nest by blending in with its surroundings. It is often possible to identify the species that built a nest by its shape, building materials, and location.

The structural integrity of the nest varies with the species and with the experience of the builder. The nest of a mourning dove is nothing more than a bunch of twigs thrown in the crotch of a branch; often, one can see daylight through it when looking

from underneath. For expert weavers like the northern oriole, however, nothing less than perfection will do, because the floor of its sack-like nest is the only thing between the eggs and a drop of 20 feet or more. Some birds will deliberately reinforce their nests. Certain warblers, hummingbirds, and blue-gray gnatcatchers incorporate spider silk, with a tensile strength higher than that of steel, into their nests, while seabirds like gulls, gannets, and cormorants will use seaweed, which is flexible when wet but rigid after it dries.

The locations and shapes of nests are also diverse. Birds will nest, literally, from the ground up; some even excavate burrows in which to raise their young. Common locations above ground include all varieties of trees and shrubs, vine tangles, brush piles, and cavities in dead trees, or snags, and stumps. Quite a few of the cavity nesters will take to artificial nest boxes, which from many standpoints are often superior to their natural sites. Floating nests anchored to aquatic vegetation are characteristic of some waterbirds. Those that have adapted well to civilization, barn swallows, European starlings, house sparrows, chimney swifts, and rock doves to name a few, prefer to nest on or in man-made structures.

To many of us, the cup-shaped nest found in trees and shrubs is the most familiar type, but there are several other basic designs. Platform nests are made of twigs, branches, and other plant matter, more or less interlaced but with no definite depression in the center or raised edges. Bowl-shaped nests are intermediate between platform nests and cup-shaped nests. Many ground-nesters lay their eggs in scrapes, simple depressions in the ground that may or may not be lined with vegetation, feathers, and other materials. Cavity nesters will excavate their own, usually in a snag, or will utilize cavities made by other birds or natural cavities in dead or dying trees or branches. Open cavities in the tops of stumps or broken-off snags are preferred by some species. Among underground nesters, burrows and rock crevices are the most common sites.

MATING – There are several types of mating strategies employed by the higher animals. Monogamy, the one most familiar to us, involves the exclusive pairing of one female and one male for a given period of time. Polygyny occurs when one male mates with several females during a short time frame; the reverse of this is polyandry, in which one female mates with several males. A few animals employ communal breeding groups, wherein each of several females in the group mates with several or all males of the group; this is known as polygynandry.

Many people tend to view nature in human terms and assume that most animals pair for life in a monogamous relationship, with a mommy and a daddy producing babies each year. In actuality, with the exception of humans, monogamy is relatively uncommon in the animal world. Most common is polygyny, of which there are several variations.

Despite the practices of the rest of the animal kingdom, most bird species (approximately nine out of ten) are monogamous. This is especially true of those birds producing altricial young, which are helpless at birth. Since the eggs are laid soon after fertilization, and since the chicks eat food caught by their parents and do not nurse, as mammals do, there is a much greater opportunity for the male to help in caring for the young birds. By sticking around in a monogamous relationship, he benefits genetically by contributing to the higher survival rate of his offspring.

Polygyny, when it does occur among birds, usually involves species whose offspring are precocial, ready upon hatching to leave the nest and fend for themselves or at least to follow their mother (as opposed to altricial young, common among songbirds, which are helpless upon hatching and must be cared for by their parents). Precocial young can be successfully reared by their mother alone, so, genetically speaking, the male benefits most by mating with many females and producing as many offspring as possible. Examples of the other breeding systems do exist among birds, but they are relatively rare.

Monogamy for birds does not necessarily mean mating for life. Courtship rituals help to establish and strengthen a pair bond between two birds early in the breeding season so that they mate only with each other. At the conclusion of the breeding

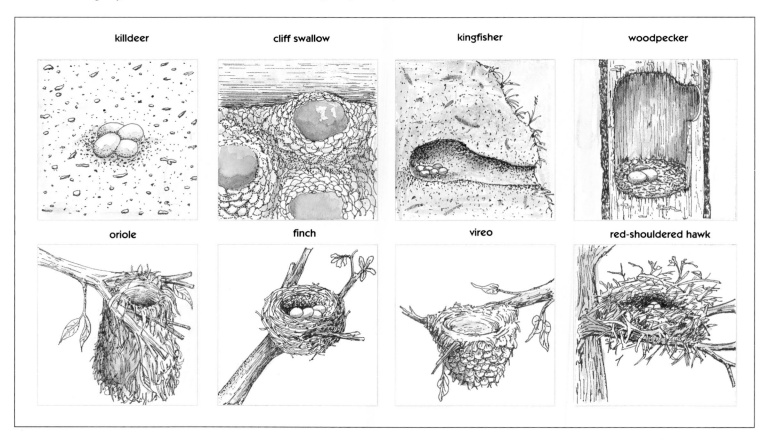

killdeer cliff swallow kingfisher woodpecker

oriole finch vireo red-shouldered hawk

Though there are many exceptions, monogamy is the general rule among birds, as typified by this screech owl family. Monogamy occurs in species when it results in the maximum number of offspring surviving to sexual maturity.

season, very often the pair bond dissolves, especially among songbirds whose life expectancy is fairly short. Remember, the name of the game is to successfully produce and rear as many offspring as possible. Once that has been accomplished, the cost of maintaining a bond between two individuals through the perils of migration or the rigors of winter is often too high, especially when there is a good chance that at least one of the pair will not survive until the next breeding season.

Long-term monogamous relationships do occur among the longer-lived species. Some, like Canada geese, are reputed to mate for life, but insufficient studies have been done to prove this theory. Upon the death of a mate, however, nearly all birds will readily accept a new partner. Often, there is a "floating" population of unmated birds ready to step in when one member of a pair dies.

FEEDING – As with most aspects of ornithology, "diverse" is the best term to describe the feeding habits of birds. If it's edible, there's probably a species of bird somewhere that eats it, within obvious physical limitations.

Not surprisingly, a large percentage of birds include arthropods and/or some form of vegetation in their diets, since these are the two most plentiful and available food sources on earth. As a class, insects alone include more species than all other living organisms combined. It is certain that birds have responded to the opportunities afforded by this great variety of available foods and evolved to include them in their diets.

In general, most birds are rather specialized feeders, and there are relatively few omnivores among them. The array of bill shapes and sizes reflects this. A cardinal with its stout, conical bill adapted for crushing seeds would find it nearly impossible to eat a mouse, let alone to catch and kill one. Likewise, the well-developed talons and hooked bill of a sharp-shinned hawk are excellent tools for dispatching and consuming small birds, but it could not make a meal out of an acorn if its life depended on it.

How birds eat is as interesting as what they eat. Gleaning, the act of searching out and gathering small bits of food piece by piece, is a common method among birds. Many sparrows are ground gleaners, taking seeds and invertebrates from the surface of soil, sand, and so on. Warblers, on the other hand, tend to be foliage gleaners, picking insects, seeds, and fruit from leaves and twigs. Bark gleaners are those who remove insects from tree trunks and branches; they include nuthatches and excavators such as woodpeckers.

Aerial feeding is also common among birds. Aerial pursuit is practiced by sharp-shinned hawks, who catch and kill small birds in mid air, while the red-tailed hawk prefers to hunt from a perch, swooping down and taking prey on the ground. The counterparts to these behaviors among insect-eaters are hawking and aerial foraging. Hawking is the act of a flycatcher, for instance, darting from a perch to catch flying insects and immediately returning, often to the same perch. Aerial foraging, practiced by swallows, is the act of capturing flying insects on a prolonged flight. Patrolling birds like bald eagles and northern harriers make sustained flights while scanning the ground, water, or trees below them in search of prey. Hummingbirds hover while gleaning nectar and insects, and hovering kestrels are a common sight as they seek a target before pouncing.

vertebrates by probing the mud or sand in or near shallow water. Dabbling and diving are practiced by waterfowl, among others. Dabbling, done mostly in shallow water, involves dipping the head underwater or tipping head down to feed. Mallards and Canada geese are familiar dabblers. Divers, like the ring-necked duck, prefer deeper water than dabblers. They swim on the water's surface but submerge and literally "fly" underwater in search of their meals. There are also high divers, like terns and kingfishers, who plunge into the water from a height, usually to catch fish.

While a bird may favor one technique over others in order to obtain its preferred fare, it is not at all unusual for a species to utilize several of the above methods, especially if it is an omnivore, one who eats a wide assortment of foods.

MIGRATION – Migration is the seasonal movement of an individual or a species from one geographical area to another, usu-

Of course, not all birds migrate. Dozens of species are able to subsist on seeds, berries, insect eggs, carrion, etc and so have no reason to risk the perils of migration. Certain others make a sort of pseudo-migration; their range compresses in the northern areas, but the bulk of the population stays put. Among the true migrators, as we will call them, two patterns of migration take place. In the first type, the species has definite summer and winter ranges, and in the fall the entire population picks up and moves en masse to their wintering grounds, and reverses the process in the spring. The other type of migration occurs when a species shifts its entire range southward in the fall and northward in the spring, but the individuals pretty much maintain their relative positions. This migratory pattern often exhibits substantial overlap between summer and winter ranges, and within this area of overlap it may appear that no migration of that species has taken place.

Great blue herons maintain a feeding territory, but nest elsewhere in treetop colonies called rookeries.

Aquatic feeders engage in some different techniques. Herons and egrets like to stalk their victims along the water's edge or stand motionless and spear those that venture too close. Probers include the great variety of shorebirds who feed upon in-

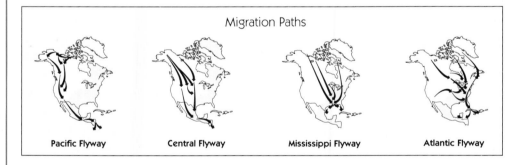

Migration Paths

Pacific Flyway   Central Flyway   Mississippi Flyway   Atlantic Flyway

ally over a sizeable distance. This definition separates the phenomenon of migration from such travel as the daily foraging flights some species make from their roosts.

Birds are the champion migrators of the world. Their ability to fly allows them to cover long distances in a fairly short period of time, and they have used this gift to their advantage. Migration enables birds to escape the rigors of the winter in their breeding territories by moving to a region of warmer temperatures and/or more food. In spring, the migrants return and disperse during the breeding season to avoid competition for food and nest sites.

Though we usually think of migration in terms of north-and-south movement, there are variations on this theme. Some species, particularly those of the more mountainous regions of the continent, migrate in a vertical direction, moving to lower elevations in the fall and returning to the high country in the spring. Other species meet their needs by migrating in a more easterly-westerly line. This pattern of migration is especially common near the coast or large lakes, where birds find milder weather and easier foraging than they would inland during winter.

Birds and You

Birdwatching

Birdwatching, or birding, as it's known among aficionados, is part of the growing national trend toward non-consumptive uses of wildlife. Such pastimes include wildlife photography, bird feeding, wildlife watching, "botanizing" (studying plants), and so on. No longer is birdwatching simply the domain of the stereotypical little old lady in a pith helmet and tennis shoes, clutching a field guide and peering through oversized binoculars into the treetops. Today's birdwatchers look just like you, your neighbor, or your boss, and they come from all walks of life, from the family who watches chickadees at their lone feeder to the retired corporate executive who now goes on birding safaris around the globe.

Birdwatching, like all fields of nature study, is a hobby that can deliver a lifetime of pleasure. No matter where you go there are birds, and you can spend a few minutes or endless enjoyable hours observing them with nothing more than your eyes, ears, and an innate curiosity. Birdwatching's pleasure can be enhanced, however, with a few carefully chosen accessories.

FIELD GUIDES – The most useful item to the birder is a good, comprehensive field guide, of which there are several on the market. Choose one with good illustrations of both sexes (when they differ) and clear descriptions denoting field marks, those characteristics that set one species apart from others. Many birders prefer field guides that are arranged taxonomically, by related groups of birds, rather than by habitat or other criteria. A given species frequently occupies more than one habitat,

Feeders need be neither complex nor large. A simple coconut shell cut in half makes a suitable food dispenser for one or two birds at a time.

and since birds don't read field guides, it is not unusual for them to show up in a place where, according to the guide, they don't "belong" at all. However, with a little practice anyone can learn the basic traits of the major bird groups and know where to turn in the field guide to make a positive identification. Even so, habitat is a useful clue for a field guide to include in its accounts, along with range maps, voice descriptions, and distinctive behavior patterns.

FIELD NOTEBOOK – As useful as a field guide is, you will learn more about birds from your own observations than you will by reading about them. Recording these observations and comparing them to various references later will fix the information in your memory; we always remember more about what we do and see than about what we read. A well-kept notebook will also help you to notice patterns of bird behavior so that you can forecast such events and be in the right place at the right time to observe them again.

Each entry in your notebook should include the date, time of day, temperature,

weather conditions, habitat, and the specific locations you visit. Record the names of the species found that day, but don't be afraid to list questionable sightings as unknown; no one can identify every single bird they see. Include notes about song, field marks, and interesting behavior. Describe the nest and eggs if you happen to see them, but do not disturb the nest in any way and do not linger near it! Remember that the welfare of the birds outweighs your thirst for knowledge. When recording observations, include numerous sketches. No matter how crude, they are invaluable as memory triggers to help you visualize details later.

OPTICAL AIDS – Because you can't always get close to the birds you want to see, a pair of good-quality binoculars will greatly enhance your birding pleasure.

Binoculars are invaluable aids in the pursuit of birds. Remember this general rule regarding binoculars: you usually get what you pay for.

There is a large assortment of models on the market today, ranging in cost from about the price of a tank of gas to a figure exceeding the monthly mortgage payment on an upper-middle-class home. While you don't need the top-of-the-line model to help you see the birds better, remember the old adage, "You get what you pay for" and buy the best that you feel you can afford. Refinements in today's compact models have made them competitive with larger glasses, and they are much easier on the neck after a day in the field.

Look for coated optics to give a brighter image, and remember that stronger is not necessarily better. While higher magnification enlarges the image you see, it also magnifies the motion of your hands, making it harder to hold the binoculars still enough to discern details. While many birders find 7× or 8× magnification ideal, some are steady enough to use 10× glasses with proficiency. The second number used to describe binoculars (7×35, 8×40, etc.) is the diameter of the objective lenses, the glass element closest to the subject. This is a good indicator of the light-gathering ability of the instrument, which determines the brightness of the image you see.

Birders who do a lot of birdwatching from a distance, as one often does with shorebirds and waterfowl, may want to invest in a good quality spotting scope. In general, the same qualities that make a good pair of binoculars will also make a good scope. Buy one with variable magnification to suit differing circumstances. In addition to the scope, you will need a sturdy tripod that extends to eye level so you don't have to stoop. A good camera store can advise you as to which one to select.

CLOTHING – The best rule of thumb here is to dress for comfort, not style. Be prepared for changes in weather, and remember that on those warm spring days it can be downright bitter by a lake, river, or along the coast. Birds respond to color, so when choosing your attire, it is best to select earth tones to avoid alarming them.

Using a blind is an effective method of watching birds at close range and observing their behavior unaffected by human presence. Blinds are nearly essential to taking frame-filling photographs of many species.

Camouflaged clothing works best if you want the birds to come to you, but you can still see plenty without dressing like a mercenary.

BIRDWATCHING – Birds are naturally wary, and while most will let you see them, rarely will they allow your close approach. This is especially true during the breeding season. Fortunately, there are several techniques you can use to bring birds closer to you.

A very effective means to achieve this is to simply sit down and wait. Just find a comfortable spot and get settled, letting yourself be absorbed by your surroundings. Though the birds can still see you, they apparently perceive you as a much lesser threat than when you're on your feet and mobile. Soon they will go back to their normal activities, and often will approach quite closely. This technique works very well with songbirds, and not well at all with most waterfowl, wading birds, and birds of prey.

An extension of the method described above is the use of a blind and/or camouflaged clothing to conceal your form. A blind may be as simple as a piece of burlap flung over you with eye holes cut out of it, or as involved as a permanent shed-like structure. Anything that hides you or breaks up your outline will work, so long as you are still. Cars make excellent blinds, even with their large windows, and they are sometimes the most practical means of obtaining close-up views, especially in many national wildlife refuges.

Tape recorders and the many excellent wildlife recordings available today make it possible to target a species and call it to you, but discretion must be used in employing this tactic. Playing the wrong song during the peak of the breeding season may agitate a territorial bird so much that it neglects its eggs or nestlings in a frenzied attempt to locate the intruder. Played at a louder than normal volume, it may intimidate more submissive individuals and cause them to desert their territory and nest. As always, the birds' welfare must take top priority.

A safer approach is to use the Audubon bird call, available from the Audubon Society, various nature centers, and bird feeding supply catalogs. Made of rosewood and pewter, it makes a variety of chipping calls that arouse songbirds' curiosity and bring them in close to investigate. You can also mimic these sounds by sucking loudly on the back of your first two fingers. Songbirds can be drawn out of dense foliage with these methods or by making a loud "psshh … psshh … psshh" sound with your lips, which some warblers find irresistible.

Feeders and Foods

One effective method of birdwatching requires that you invite birds to your home instead of going afield in search of them. Providing food, water, and shelter on your property can result in a pleasing assortment of species frequenting your surroundings throughout the year. By positioning feeders so that your favorite windows provide clear views of them, your house becomes a giant bird blind, and from within you can spy on the daily activities of your feathered neighbors.

The prices of feeders sold in retail stores may seem prohibitive, but don't let this dissuade you from setting up your own feeding station. Feeders can be made simply and inexpensively using natural materials or scrap lumber and other items found around the house. Don't worry if you're not an ace carpenter; the birds really don't care what your feeders look like, only that they contain food. In fact, you'll be amazed at how much better any feeder looks with a cardinal, evening grosbeak, or other colorful species perched upon it.

There are four major feeding niches around any home that should be filled in order to attract the greatest variety of birds. The upper level should include hanging feeder and high post feeders, the middle level is complete with low post feeders and bench-level platform feeders, and the lower level should have feeders at ground level or seed scattered directly on the ground. The fourth zone, tree trunks and branches, is the domain of woodpeckers and nuthatches, so the feeders need to be mounted on these surfaces.

Birds that frequent feeders enjoy a variety of foods, but there are a few staples that will satisfy the majority of them. Sunflower seed is one of these. It has a higher fat content than other common grains, which may account for its popularity, especially in winter when every calorie counts. Opinions vary, but the black oil sunflower seed seems to be more favored by birds than the larger striped variety. It has a higher fat content, its thin hull is opened easily, and small birds find its smaller size easier to manipulate with their bills and feet.

Beef suet is another popular item. You can use it straight from the butcher, but most experts recommend rendering it in a double-boiler in order to eliminate the stringiness. There are also commercially available suet cakes, most of which are impregnated with one or more types of seed. Birds like them, but their main advantage is convenience. Suet is especially attractive to insect eaters like woodpeckers and nuthatches.

Other foods receiving favorable feathered reviews are white proso millet, peanut hearts, niger seed, and cracked corn. While niger seed does not appeal to a broad spectrum of birds, it will bring finches in droves, especially American goldfinches. Cracked corn is readily accepted by a number of species, but it tends to lure undesirable visitors such as squirrels, house sparrows, brown-headed cowbirds, and common grackles, among others. Shrewd birdwatchers can use this knowledge to their advantage by establishing a feeding station featuring corn in a remote area in order to keep the riffraff away from their other feeders.

Beware of the commercially prepared wild bird seed mixtures. Studies have shown that these often contain fairly large percentages of grains ignored by wild birds. You will attract more birds for the buck if you experiment with different seed types and then offer your birds what you know they prefer. In any case, buying in bulk at a

Tree swallows will readily use nest boxes of a proper size in suitable locations, and reward nearby homeowners by consuming vast numbers of flying insects.

feed mill is far less expensive than purchasing those little five or ten pound bags in retail stores.

Supplemental foods that may attract more unusual birds to your feeding station include fruits, melon seeds, peanut butter, and nutmeats that have been freed from thick-hulled varieties like pecans, acorns, walnuts, and hickory nuts. A word of caution about feeding peanut butter: never offer pure peanut butter, for it is known to clog the esophagus of birds, causing them to choke to death. Always mix about 1 part peanut butter with 5 parts cornmeal to prevent such a tragedy and extend your expensive peanut butter supply.

Other supplemental foods may be provided by landscape plantings. This type of landscaping is sometimes called wildlife gardening, and is growing in popularity among American homeowners. Aside from encouraging wildlife visits, a well-planned natural landscape can be very attractive and requires much less maintenance than the traditional manicured lawn and formal gardens. Sure winners among bird-attracting plants are flowering dogwood, red mulberry, common chokecherry, Russian olive, blueberries, flowering crabapples, and American mountain ash. There are many others that are too numerous to mention here, and plant selections will vary considerably with climate. Also, don't forget that many of the so-called "weeds" produce seeds attractive to birds.

Birds need grit in order for their digestive system to function properly, and you can provide this at your feeding station. Coarse sand, fine gravel, or the grit available in pet stores will meet this need when placed in a small bowl near your feeders. Birds are also fond of salt. The coarse type may be offered separately or mixed with the grit.

Many well-meaning bird lovers will spare no expense in feeding their feathered friends, but overlook one of their most basic necessities: water. This is a real hardship faced by birds, especially in the north country during winter, when most water is locked up as ice and snow. Birds also love

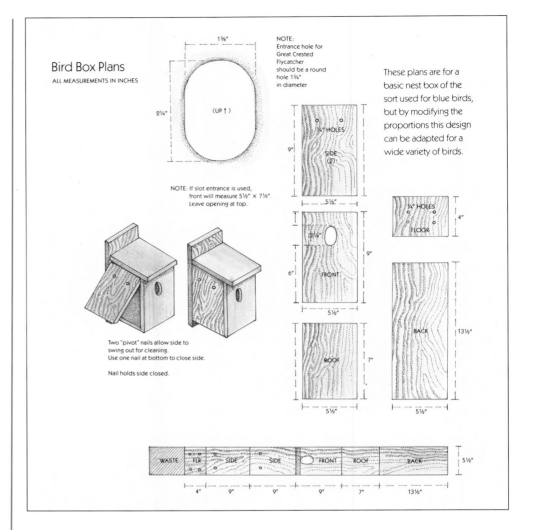

to bathe in water, an act that plays an important role in feather maintenance. Keep at least one birdbath filled at your feeding station at all times. A thermostatically-controlled heater is inexpensive to operate and will keep your birdbath ice-free on the most bitter winter day.

Nest Sites

Supplying food and water, two of life's necessities, will bring many birds to visit your home. Furnishing nest sites will encourage some of them to become residents, and there are two basic ways to do this for the smaller birds. One is by erecting nest boxes, which are readily accepted by many cavity-nesters. You can buy nest boxes already assembled, but it's fun to make your own, and it can be done with scrap lumber and only the most elementary carpentry skills. There are so many possible birdhouse

designs, but the basic tall box-shape commonly seen can be adapted to suit most backyard cavity nesters by altering its dimensions and the size of the entrance. It is important that any nest box be well-ventilated, allow for drainage, and have a door that opens to facilitate cleaning before the nesting season begins.

Another way to encourage nesting on your property is to keep your landscape as natural as possible. A diversity of native plants, especially trees and shrubs of different densities and heights, will meet the needs of a lot of species, and an unmown area might even encourage ground-nesters. If you own a sizeable lot and can stand their slightly unkempt appearance, brush piles are extremely attractive to numerous species. Consider leaving snags (dead trees) standing for the woodpeckers and other cavity nesters, provided that there is no danger of their falling.

Species Directory

The Species Directory includes accounts of 128 of the more easily seen North American birds. For species that exhibit marked differences in plumage between the sexes, males have been illustrated whenever possible, since they are usually easier to identify than females.

Each account also provides details concerning the bird's habitat preferences. food preferences, nest location, and nest type. These generally illustrate the most common criteria for each species, but remember that, since birds don't read about themselves in field guides, there are bound to be exceptions. Also listed for each species are length from tip of bill to tip of tail, and wingspan for the larger birds with slower wingbeats. These measurements represent the average of those recorded for live adult males captured and hand-held in natural positions. They tend to be substantially less than those derived from lifeless birds listed in most field guides, but they more accurately represent what you as an observer are likely to see in the field.

Bird range throughout North America

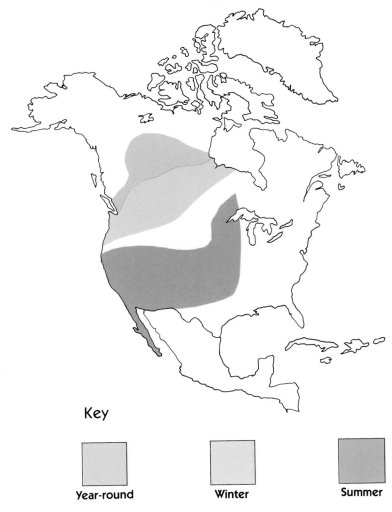

Key

Year-round

Winter

Summer

ORDER PODICIPEDIFORMES,
FAMILY PODICIPEDIDAE

Pied-billed Grebe

Podilymbus podiceps

Habitat: pond, lake, marsh.
Food: fish, aquatic invertebrates
Nest Location: floating
Nest Type: plate
Wingspan: 22″
Length: 9″

Small and unobtrusive, the pied-billed grebe is the most common grebe of North America. It feeds on small fish, aquatic insects, and crustaceans, and is especially fond of crayfish. When frightened, it can compress the air from its layer of feathers and slowly sink out of sight in an inconspicuous fashion, only to surface again in the protective cover of shoreline reeds.

Pied-billed grebes are one of the species known to carry their young on their backs while swimming. There is a definite advantage to this behavior, as the species produces small broods and cannot afford many losses to aquatic predators that thin out the larger broods of other waterfowl.

In summer, this plain-looking brown bird bears a black throat and a black ring around

its chicken-like bill, field marks which are absent in winter.

Distasteful as it sounds, grebes have been observed to eat their own feathers. It is believed that to help the bird digest fish bones by padding the sharp ends and by slowing down the digestive process, thus allowing more time for the bones to dissolve before passing into the intestine.

ORDER PELICANIFORMES,
FAMILY PHALACROCORACIDAE

Double-crested Cormorant

Phalacrocorax penicillatus

Habitat: lake, pond, river, swamp, coastal.
Food: fish, aquatic invertebrates
Nest Location: ground, trees 6-150′
Nest Type: plate
Wingspan: 50″
Length: 27″

The primary food of these primitive birds is fish, which they pursue underwater and catch in their pouched bills. Such good fishermen are they that, in China and Japan,

it is a centuries-old practice to use cormorants to catch fish. On the fishing grounds, rings are placed around the necks of leashed cormorants, preventing the birds from swallowing their prey. After each catch, the cormorant is retrieved by its leash and the fish is removed. The ring is removed periodically to allow the bird to feed itself.

The large, silent, V-shaped flocks of migrating double-crested cormorants are often mistaken for geese by casual observers. The crests for which it is named are rarely visible, but the species is easily distinguished by its orange throat pouch and its habit of swimming low in the water with its hooked bill tilted upward. Cormorants are gifted with the ability to compress air from their feathers, which allows them to sink inconspicuously into the water to avoid detection. "Cormorant" is a French derivative of the Latin name "corvus marinus", which translates to "sea crow."

ORDER ANSERIFORMES, FAMILY ANATIDAE

Canada Goose

Branta canadensis

Habitat: lake, pond, marsh, field, coastal
Food: grain, seeds, grass, aquatic vegetation, terrestrial invertebrates, aquatic invertebrates
Nest Location: ground, artificial structure
Nest Type: scrape
Wingspan: 68″
Length: 25″

Canada geese, whose lyrical honking was once dubbed "goose music" by the great American conservationist Aldo Leopold, are one of the premier North American game birds. Goose music and their familiar "V" formations as they fly toward seasonal destinations have become the hallmarks of spring and autumn migration.

Canada geese, often mispronounced "Canadian geese", nest near water and sleep on the water when not nesting, but during the day they often commute to nearby farm fields to feed on waste grain, insects, and grass. An interesting aspect of their social behavior is their posting of "sentinels". While the rest of the flock is feeding, preening, or sleeping, one or more sentinels are always at attention with their heads erect, alertly surveying their surroundings. When the sentinel's watch is over, it lowers its head and another goose instantly assumes lookout duty.

Flocks break up after spring migration, as mated pairs seek suitable nest sites. Pairs are reputed to mate for life, although this has not been conclusively proven and exceptions have been observed. The downy, yellowish green goslings are precocial, immediately following their parents to the water and plunging in after hatching. In late summer, families begin to congregate in flocks for the fall migration. Frequently they gather on large lawns or golf courses to molt, causing quite a nuisance.

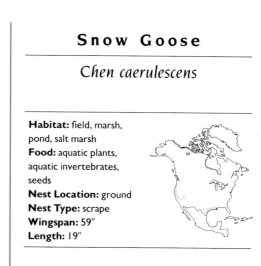

Canadian geese.

Snow geese in flight.

Snow Goose

Chen caerulescens

Habitat: field, marsh, pond, salt marsh
Food: aquatic plants, aquatic invertebrates, seeds
Nest Location: ground
Nest Type: scrape
Wingspan: 59″
Length: 19″

When flocks of migrating geese descend upon farm lands in the hope of salvaging the waste grain missed by the last harvest, the uninitiated bird watcher may wonder if the white individuals sometimes mingling with Canada geese are albinos. Veteran birders, though, will immediately guess that these are snow geese, and upon closer inspection, they are usually proven correct.

As a species, snow geese include a dark phase, formerly known as the blue goose and once considered a separate species. The dark phase shows the same white head and throat as its mostly-white counterpart, but its body is dark gray. Black wing tips and a pink bill with black "lips" set the snow goose apart from most other white waterfowl. In flight, flocks of snow geese usually fly in a "U" formation.

Snow geese nest about as far north as they possibly could, on the Arctic tundra along the coast of Hudson Bay and the Arctic Ocean. They nest in colonies of up to tens of thousands, and the female usually returns to the colony where she hatched, an amazing feat in a region nearly devoid of landmarks. At these latitudes, larger birds like the snow goose, with long incubation periods and slow maturation, are totally dependent upon the whims of the climate. In a late spring, the species may skip nesting altogether if there is not enough time for the young to mature. The early onset of winter may strand many young snow geese still unable to fly.

Mallard

Anas platyrhynchos

Habitat: pond, freshwater marsh, swamp, river, lake
Food: seeds, aquatic plants
Nest Location: ground
Nest Type: scrape
Wingspan: 36″
Length: 16″

Perhaps the most familiar of North American ducks, the mallard drake is recognized by its metallic-green head, white neck-ring, and chestnut-brown breast. The hen, a mottled brown color, shares the male's metallic-blue speculum.

Mallards are dabbling ducks which feed in shallow water by tipping up, as opposed to the diving habits of some other ducks. They belong to a group sometimes called "puddle ducks" for their habit of frequenting bodies of water which are often little more than puddles. The forward position of their feet and their relatively large wings make vertical take-offs possible, compared with diving ducks that gain momentum by running over the water's surface and therefore need a fairly large stretch of water to become airborne.

Black Duck

Anas rubripes

Habitat: pond, freshwater marsh, river, lake, estuary, tidal mud flats
Food: aquatic invertebrates, seeds, aquatic plants
Nest Location: ground
Nest Type: scrape
Wingspan: 36″
Length: 16″

So named for the drake's dark-brown plumage, black ducks are best identified by their metallic-violet wing patch and the white lining under the wing which is visible in flight. The hen is similar in appearance to a female mallard, and the two species share many behavioral traits as well.

Like most ducklings, the young of black ducks are precocial, following their mother to water almost immediately after hatching and are able to swim and feed themselves. Though they stay close to protective cover, the ducklings are vulnerable to underwater predators such as snapping turtles, pickerel, and pike. To compensate for the losses as a result of these predators, black ducks lay a clutch of 8-10 eggs to ensure that some will reach maturity.

American Widgeon

Mareca americana

Habitat: marsh, lake, pond
Food: aquatic plants, grass, grain, aquatic invertebrates
Nest Location: ground
Nest Type: scrape
Wingspan: 34″
Length: 14″

American widgeon are the shakedown artists of waterfowl. While they can and do dive, these wary birds prefer to spend their time in the company of other species of diving ducks such as redheads and canvasbacks waiting at the surface and snatching morsels of food away from the other ducks as they surface. They also feed in grain fields and meadows, where they eat waste grain and graze on tender shoots.

They are recognized in flight by their large white shoulder patches. At rest, the male is distinguished by a green ear patch and by his white crown, producing the illusion that resulted in its other common name, "baldpate". The female is a rather nondescript, mottled brown with a gray head and whitish belly. Both have pale blue bills and feet.

Northern Shoveler

Spatula clypeata

Habitat: marsh, pond
Food: aquatic plants, aquatic invertebrates, seeds
Nest Location: ground
Nest Type: scrape
Wingspan: 31″
Length: 14″

With its rich coloration and bold markings, the northern shoveler would be an extraordinarily handsome duck were it not for its comically large bill. Nevertheless, its oversized mandibles serve it very well as it filters small animals, seeds and plant bits from the water's surface and from the bottom ooze. Because of its feeding habits and its preference for stagnant bodies of water, the shoveler is especially vulnerable to botulism, a fatal food poisoning caused by bacteria of oxygen-poor environments.

Shovelers are among the first waterfowl to arrive on their winter range in the fall and one of the last to leave in the spring. Aside from the large bill, the principal identifying characteristic of female shovelers, the drakes are identifiable by their combination of a green head, white breast, chestnut belly and flanks, pale blue shoulder patches, and a green speculum, or wing patch, on each wing.

Green-winged Teal

Anas carolinensis

Habitat: marsh, pond, stream
Food: seeds, grain, grass, aquatic invertebrates
Nest Location: ground
Nest Type: scrape
Wingspan: 24″
Length: 10.5″

Green-winged teal are among the fastest-flying ducks, and are therefore popular game birds. To feed, they usually dip their head under the surface or tip head down, a behavior known as dabbling. They are smaller than other dabbling ducks and therefore feed in shallower water, minimizing competition for the same foods. With their relatively large wings and the forward position of their feet, green-winged teal are among the "puddle ducks" that can take off vertically, rather than running across the water's surface. Partly for this reason, they prefer smaller bodies of water.

The smallest of these puddle ducks, green-winged teal migrate in moderate to large flocks that fly in tight formation, executing sharp twists, turns, and dives in unison. The drake is easily recognized by the metallic green eye patch on a cinnamon head, the metallic green wing patch or speculum, and the vertical white stripe in his side. The hen is a mottle brown with the same green speculum.

Wood Duck

Aix sponsa

Habitat: swamp, marsh, pond, river
Food: seeds, grain, fruit, aquatic invertebrates, terrestrial invertebrates
Nest Location: snag, 1-30', nest box
Nest Type: cavity
Wingspan: 28"
Length: 13.5"

Undoubtedly the most beautiful of all our native waterfowl, the wood duck's population was reduced to a perilously low level in the late 1800s by over-hunting and the destruction of nesting habitat. Protected by law and bolstered by the ambitious effort by sportsmen and birdwatchers, their numbers have increased to the point where they are now one of the more common ducks in the Northeast.

Wood ducks are commonly found in swamps and in the ponds, streams and river bottomlands of wooded areas, although they may be seen in marshes during migration. They are particularly fond of acorns which drop into the water from adjacent oak trees.

The rainbow hues of the drake are difficult to describe. He displays a bright orange bill, red eyes, an erratic white facial pattern, and a swept-back crest on his iridescent green head. A wine-colored breast, pale yellow flanks, and blue, purple, and burgundy wing feathers complete his spectrum. The female, though much duller, possesses similar hues on her wings, as well as a white eye patch.

Common Merganser

Mergus merganser

Habitat: lake, pond, river
Food: fish, aquatic invertebrates, amphibians
Nest Location: deciduous tree <50', bank, ground
Nest Type: cavity
Wingspan: 37"
Length: 18"

The common merganser's serrate, or saw-toothed, bill is uniquely adapted for catching and holding on to slippery fish, its primary food. They require clear water for pursuing and catching prey, hence they prefer to nest in the cool, clear lakes and rivers of boreal and western forests. While they will choose to nest in tree cavities when available, common merganser nests on the ground under dense cover, in rock crevices, earthen banks, and in hollows under tree roots are not uncommon.

Mergansers were once persecuted because it was believed that they decimated gamefish populations. Today, it is understood that they benefit fish by inhibiting overpopulation and allowing the surviving individuals to reach larger sizes.

The common merganser is slimmer than the common goldeneye, which it resembles in plumage. Its slender bright-reddish-orange bill, slightly hooked at the tip, is one of the best field marks. The male's green head may appear black, and contrasts sharply with the white breast and sides. The female common merganser has a crested rufous head and neck, sharply contrasting with its white throat and breast. Both sexes have large, square white wing patches.

Ring-necked Duck

Aythya collaris

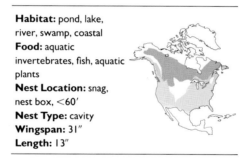

Habitat: lake, pond, swamp, bog, marsh
Food: seeds, aquatic plants, aquatic invertebrates
Nest Location: ground
Nest Type: scrape
Wingspan: 28″
Length: 12″

These divers are partial to acid lakes and ponds in wooded areas. Ring-necked ducks and certain other ducks often migrate and winter in large flocks of a single species, called *rafts*. They often migrate only as far south as is necessary to find open water, wintering in the estuaries and lakes in the middle latitudes of North America.

Their name is something of a misnomer. It has been suggested that the ring-necked duck should actually be called the ring-*billed* duck, as the white ring around its bill is a much more evident field mark than the chestnut collar around its neck, which is visible only at close range. Males also sport a yellow eye, a vertical white stripe just in front of their wing, and a solid black back. The females are a nondescript brown, distinguished only by their white eye-ring and whitish ring around the bill.

Common Goldeneye

Bucephala clangula

Habitat: pond, lake, river, swamp, coastal
Food: aquatic invertebrates, fish, aquatic plants
Nest Location: snag, nest box, <60′
Nest Type: cavity
Wingspan: 31″
Length: 13″

Goldeneyes are sometimes called "whistlers" because of the whistling sound produced by their wing feathers in flight. They prefer fresh water, but will migrate to the coasts when inland waters are frozen. Common goldeneyes nest mainly in the lakes of the boreal forest, and therefore are seen in the lower 48 states mostly in winter or during migration. They seem to prefer nesting in the open-topped, or "bucket" cavities of a broken snag rather than enclosed cavities, although they will use either. Aquatic invertebrates compose approximately three-quarters of their diet.

The best field marks of the male common goldeneye are the large white cheek patch on its glossy green head and the large white wing patches in flight. Females are gray with a brown head, white collar, and white wing patches visible in flight.

Bufflehead

Bucephala albeola

Habitat: lake, river, ocean
Food: invertebrates, aquatic plants
Nest Location: snag, 2-10′, bank
Nest Type: cavity or burrow
Wingspan: 24″
Length: 10″

Our smallest duck has a very large namesake. The bufflehead is supposedly named for the buffalo because the shape and proportion of its head resembles that of the majestic plains animal. All in all, however, the bufflehead must definitely be considered the more attractive of the two, and it's a much better diver, too!

The male bufflehead has snow-white underparts and a black back. A large white patch arches from eye to eye across the back of his head, interrupting an iridescent rainbow of a hood. Very drab in comparison, the female may be recognized by her size, an elliptical white cheek patch, and her association with the drake during the spring.

ORDER FALCONIFORMES,
FAMILY CATHARTIDAE

Turkey Vulture

Cathartes aura

Habitat: deciduous forest, field, grassland
Food: carrion
Nest Location: cliffs, snags
Nest Type: none
Wingspan: 72"
Length: 25"

A face only a mother could love – that is probably the best way to describe a turkey vulture. Homely though they are, they perform an invaluable ecological service. Vultures are nature's garbage collectors, seeking and removing dead mammals and birds that have met their demise by whatever means. In this way they participate in the recycling of nutrients through the eco-system while removing diseased carcasses that could pose health threats to wildlife populations. In populated areas, vultures frequently find their cuisine along roads.

Perhaps the most remarkable aspect of turkey vultures is their ability to soar on the slightest updrafts for hours on end without a single wingbeat. Once they gain minimal altitude after takeoff, their wide, expansive wings catch thermals or forced updrafts and allow them to adjust their altitude at will by simply manipulating their wing positions relative to the air currents.

Another unusual trait of turkey vultures is their well-developed sense of smell, unlike many other birds, which possess rather poor olfactory abilities. A series of experiments demonstrated that turkey vultures were consistently able to locate hidden animal bait while ignoring a stuffed mule deer which was well-exposed and correctly positioned.

Male and female turkey vultures are identical. A mature T.V., as they are known among birders, has a small red head devoid of feathers. The naked head is an evolutionary adaptation benefiting their health and hygiene. Hard-to-clean head feathers would become a matted haven for bacteria and parasites as the bird fed on the gooey innards of its "prey". In flight, turkey vultures are easily distinguished from other large, dark birds by their uptilted wings held in a shallow "V", or dihedral, position.

Sharp-shinned Hawk

Accipiter striatus

Habitat: coniferous forest, deciduous forest, thicket
Food: birds
Nest Location: conifer, deciduous trees, 10-60'
Nest Type: plate
Wingspan: 21"
Length: 10.5"

With superior maneuverability afforded by their short but strong wings and long, rudder-like tails, sharp-shinned hawks are superbly designed for the pursuit and capture of their favorite prey, small songbirds. They are very aggressive hunters, and have been known to finish a chase on foot when their prey took refuge under dense brush.

Sharp-shinned hawks are the smallest and commonest of three species of accipiters native to North America. Accipiters are characterized by their flight pattern, a series of short wingbeats interrupted by periodic glides. The squared end of their tail is a primary factor distinguishing them from the slightly larger Cooper's hawk. An effective aid in identifying sharp-shinned hawks is the saying, "Flap, flap, sail; long square tail." The sexes bear similar plumage, but females are larger than males, so the three species of accipiters overlap in size. Like the other accipiters, mature sharp-shinned hawks have red eyes and solid slate-gray backs. They have horizontal rufous barring on their breasts.

Northern Harrier

Circus cyaneus

Habitat: field, marsh, grassland
Food: small mammals, small vertebrates, insects
Nest Location: ground, shrub <5'
Nest Type: plate
Wingspan: 42"
Length: 16.5"

Northern harriers, formerly known as marsh hawks, are usually seen coursing low over meadows or marshes, quartering the area like a bird dog in search of game. They rely on their quick reflexes and upon the element of surprise in order to secure their meals. Northern harriers glide with their long, rounded wings held upward in a shallow "V", or dihedral, position, just as turkey vultures do.

This is one of only three North American raptors to exhibit a marked difference in plumage between the sexes. Mature males are pale gray, while the females have dark-brown backs and streaked breasts. Both possess a large, conspicuous white rump patch. It is believed that their disk-shaped faces serve to amplify the sound waves reaching their ears, facilitating the location of prey when the harriers cruise at an altitude of seven feet or less.

Red-tailed Hawk

Buteo jamaicensis

Habitat: deciduous forest, forest edge, field, grassland, desert
Food: small mammals, birds, reptiles, insects
Nest Location: deciduous trees 15-70', cliffs
Nest Type: plate
Wingspan: 48"
Length: 18"

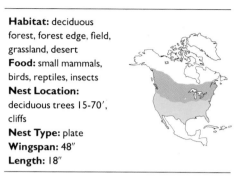

Individual red-tailed hawks vary greatly in plumage, from pale to very dark or melanistic. They also exhibit the highest rate of albinism of any North American raptor. Except for albinos, red-tails are easily identified by their rufous tail feathers. All but the darkest individuals have a dark band of feathers across the belly (the "belly band") which contrasts with a lighter breast.

Though they nest in the forest, red-tailed hawks generally hunt in open territory such as farmlands and highway medians. They prefer to hunt from a perch, studiously scanning the ground for the motion of a rodent. When red-tails do hunt from the air, they will often turn into the wind and tilt their wings just so, so that lift equals gravity and forward glide equals wind speed, allowing them to hang motionless for long periods. A degree of cooperative hunting has been observed between red-tailed hawks, where one hawk makes a fake pass at a squirrel on a tree while its mate approaches from the opposite direction. The squirrel dodges around the tree trunk only to be picked off by the second bird.

Red-tailed hawks and great horned owls form an ecological analog, two unrelated species that occupy similar niches. Since the owl is nocturnal and the hawk is diurnal, they are able to coexist in the same area without direct competition from each other.

Red-shouldered Hawk

Buteo lineatus

Habitat: riparian forest, swamp, deciduous forest
Food: reptiles, amphibians, small mammals, birds, terrestrial invertebrates, aquatic invertebrates
Nest Location: deciduous tree, 20-60'
Nest Type: plate
Wingspan: 40"
Length: 16"

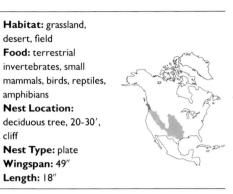

Red-shouldered hawks have carved their primary ecological niche out of the swamps and river bottomlands of eastern North America, where they experience little competition from the closely-related species of their range, red-tailed hawks and broad-winged hawks of the upland forests. Naturally, their diet consists largely of animals common to such areas, such as snakes, turtles, frogs, crayfish, and even fish.

Narrow white bands on a dark tail, rufous shoulder patches, and uniformly reddish underparts are all field marks of the red-shouldered hawk, but the most easily distinguished from a distance are the wing "windows", translucent areas of the outer wings where sunlight seems to shine through in flight.

Broad-winged Hawk

Buteo platypterus

Habitat: deciduous forest, mixed forest
Food: reptiles, small mammals, amphibians, insects
Nest Location: deciduous trees, 30-50'
Nest Type: plate
Wingspan: 33"
Length: 13"

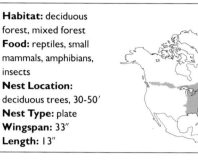

Though fairly common, these woodland raptors are rather quiet and inconspicuous, spending most of their time beneath the forest canopy, and are therefore often overlooked. During the fall migration, however, the extent of the broad-winged hawk population becomes quite evident as they gather in swirling groups, called "kettles", that number from less than a dozen to more than a thousand. A more impressive scene in nature is hard to imagine when one witnesses one of these giant kettles whirling and churning their way to the top of a thermal updraft and then setting their wings and gliding southward in a massive stream in search of the next thermal.

The smallest of the North American buteos, or soaring hawks, mature broad-winged hawks are readily identified by the prominent black and white bands on their tails and by their white underwings with contrasting black-tipped primary feathers. Both of these field marks are most evident in flight.

Swainson's Hawk

Buteo swainsoni

Habitat: grassland, desert, field
Food: terrestrial invertebrates, small mammals, birds, reptiles, amphibians
Nest Location: deciduous tree, 20-30', cliff
Nest Type: plate
Wingspan: 49"
Length: 18"

Swainson's hawks hold the distance record for migratory birds of prey, nesting as far north as Alaska but wintering in Argentina, a round trip of up to 17,000 miles. Their summer range includes not only the mountainous West but also the Great Plains, where treeless expanses may force them to build nests on cliff ledges. They are gregarious birds during migration, often moving in great swarming "kettles" of thousands of birds as they ride thermal updrafts to gain altitude.

This is an attractive raptor, especially in the light color phase, which has buffy underparts, a terminal black tail band, a white throat and brow, and a rich brown collar on the upper breast. In the dark phase, it is uniformly dark except for the white brow and throat. In agricultural areas, they have the rather undignified but very nutritious habit of trailing after tractors and snapping up prodigious numbers of grasshoppers and crickets stirred up in its wake.

American Kestrel

Falco sparverius

Habitat: field, grassland, desert, suburban, urban
Food: terrestrial invertebrates, small mammals, reptiles, amphibians
Nest Location: snag 12-80′, nest box, cliff
Nest Type: cavity
Wingspan: 21″
Length: 8.5″

The American kestrel, formerly known as a sparrow hawk, is the smallest of our North American falcons. They are swift fliers that rarely soar. Along with the typical falcon field marks of long, streamlined wings and a long, narrow tail, kestrels are exquisitely marked with an ornate facial pattern and relatively bright colors for a raptor. Their rufous back and tail are diagnostic, as are the bluish-gray wings of the male. Females have rufous wings.

Kestrels are hunters of open ground. They are fond of perching on telephone wires and scanning the ground for their favorite prey, grasshoppers and small rodents. Kestrels also hunt by hovering over treeless terrain on furious but shallow wingbeats and dropping swiftly onto their target. They are nearly always solitary, even during the breeding season when the male spends most of his time hunting while the female remains close to the nest, relying on her mate for food.

Wild Turkey

Meleagris gallopavo

Habitat: deciduous, mixed, coniferous, & riparian forests, swamps
Food: seeds, nuts, fruit, insects, terrestrial invertebrates, reptiles, amphibians
Nest Location: ground
Nest Type: scrape
Wingspan: 60″
Length: 34″

Stately in appearance and nominated by Ben Franklin to become this country's national symbol, this bronzed bird is the undisputed ruler of the forest floor among woodland birds. In courtship displays, the male, called a gobbler, can be imposing with tail fanned, plumage erect; and the wattles of his naked head infused with red and purplish-blue color. Mature gobblers also sport a "beard", modified hair-like feathers protruding from the breast, the function of which is unknown. Females, or hens, are similar in appearance but lack the beard and brightly colored wattles. Gobblers are polygynous, using their impressive strutting displays and calls to attract and keep a harem. After mating, harems break up and each female cares for the eggs and raises her offspring alone. Turkeys are omnivorous, but they are particularly fond of mast crops like acorns and beech nuts, and are more common in forests with many oak or beech trees.

Wild turkeys rank as one of the wariest of woodland birds, to which any hunter or photographer who has ever stalked them can attest. They are often seen running away after they have already spied you. Deceptively swift for their size, turkeys can sprint at 18 miles per hour; they rely on running to escape danger. Though they are not strong fliers, once airborne they can glide at speeds up to 55 mph.

Gone from most of their range by the mid-nineteenth century due to a combination of habitat loss, hunting pressures, and predation, wild turkeys have made a strong comeback through the wise management practices and aggressive reintroduction programs of various state wildlife agencies. Their population today is estimated at roughly 3 million birds and growing in the United States. One can often tell that a flock has been in the area by the "scratchings" they leave, areas of forest floor where the leaves have been shoved aside by these omnivores as they search for food.

ORDER GALLIFORMES,
FAMILY TETRAONIDAE

Ruffed Grouse

Bonasa umbellus

Habitat: deciduous or
mixed forest
Food: plants, seeds, fruit,
insects, terrestrial
invertebrates
Nest Location: ground
Nest Type: scrape
Length: 14"

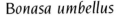

Among northern folks this bird is also known as a "pa'tridge", but it belongs to a different family than the gray partridge introduced from Europe to western agricultural lands. Woodland explorers usually first become aware of a ruffed grouse in the vicinity when it explodes into takeoff from a nearby hiding place, dodging through the trees on whirring wings.

The courtship display of the male ruffed grouse includes an erect black ruff around its neck, for which the bird is named, and a beautifully fanned tail. This species occurs in two color phases, gray and red; the red phase is actually reddish-brown.

These upland game birds are most notable for their spring-time drumming, a throbbing boom that begins slowly and accelerates in tempo into a drum roll, echoing through the forest and telling all the world that a virile male ruffed grouse is present and available. Drumming is performed on a favorite drumming log, stump, or other vantage point; the sound is produced as the male, standing erect with tail braced against the log, vigorously beats his cupped wings at his sides. Drumming takes the place of song in courtship and in asserting territoriality. Ruffed grouse are polygynous; the male claims a breeding territory and commences drumming to attract as many females as possible, who may or may not nest on the male's territory but raise their precocial broods by themselves.

Sharp-tailed Grouse

Pediocetes phasianellus

Habitat: grassland,
sagebrush, thickets,
savannah, forest clearings,
coniferous forest
Food: plants, nuts, fruit,
seeds, terrestrial
invertebrates
Nest Location: ground
Nest Type: scrape
Length: 15"

Sharp-tailed grouse exhibit a distinct lack of modesty when it comes to their sex lives. Males gather at leks, communal ancestral breeding grounds, to perform courtship dances in an attempt to lure females. Each male claims a small territory within the lek from which to display, with the more dominant individuals occupying the areas closest to the center of the lek.

The enthusiasm of his displays and his location within the lek indicate a male's fitness as a mate, and females make their selections accordingly. Males are promiscuous, mating with as many females as possible; females, in turn, leave the lek after they are fertilized, possibly by several males, and raise their brood of precocial chicks alone. The use of leks, which affords dominant males the opportunity to mate with many more females than they otherwise could, has evolved mostly among species of prairies and other open terrain, where predators can be spotted from a distance.

Though they are swift fliers, sharp-tailed grouse prefer to remain on the ground. During the warmer months they partake of succulent plants, berries, nuts, seeds, and insects, but when winter sweeps away the insects and herbaceous plants and covers their other foods with snow, these birds take to the trees to feast on buds until

spring arrives with its bounty.

Sharp-tailed grouse are quite chicken-like in appearance. Their white breast is mottled with brownish marks, a pattern that reverses itself on the back. In flight, they show white outer tail feathers. During their dancing displays, males inflate purple air sacs on either side of their necks.

ORDER GALLIFORMES,
FAMILY PHASIANIDAE

Common Bobwhite

Colinus virginianus

Habitat: field, prairie, thicket
Food: plants, fruit, seeds, terrestrial invertebrates
Nest Location: ground
Nest Type: scrape
Length: 8″

The sprightly little bobwhite has actually named itself, proclaiming its identity in clearly whistled tones over and over every spring. The sexes are similar in appearance: chunky, mottled reddish-brown, with rounded wings and a gray tail. The throat and eye stripe of males are white, but the same regions on female birds are replaced by a buffy color.

After the nesting season, quail gather into groups of two or three dozen birds called coveys. Upon sensing danger, the birds freeze, relying on their camouflaged plumage to avoid detection. If the intruder moves into their safety zone, the entire covey explodes into the air in a flurry of wing beats and scatters in all directions. The birds then call to locate each other. Another benefit of group life comes in the evening. The covey assembles in a circular pattern with heads outward. This formation conserves body heat and enables the group to spot danger from 360 degrees.

Ring-necked Pheasant

Phasianus colchicus

Habitat: thicket, field, forest edge, grassland
Food: seeds, grain, fruit, terrestrial invertebrates, reptiles, amphibians
Nest Location: ground
Nest Type: scrape
Length: 27″

This bird, introduced from Asia in 1887, adapted so well that it became one of North America's premier game species, but its numbers have declined in the last few decades due to habitat loss and changes in agricultural practices. The early summer mowing of alfalfa and cool-weather grasses for hay occurs at the peak of the breeding season, destroying nests, chicks, and incubating adults.

The ring-necked pheasant's name is derived from the white collar of the male, who is otherwise decorated with intricate feather patterns in an iridescent rainbow of hues. His brilliant green head and the scarlet wattles around his eyes are also characteristic. Both sexes have very long, pointed tail feathers, but the plumage of the female is otherwise a much duller, mottled brown. Though capable of swift bursts of flight, pheasants are relatively weak fliers, preferring to escape danger by running through concealing grass and brush.

ORDER CICONIIFORMES,
FAMILY ARDEIDAE

Great Egret

Casmerodius albus

Habitat: freshwater marsh, salt marsh, pond, tidal flats
Food: fish, amphibians, reptiles, aquatic invertebrates
Nest Location: deciduous trees & shrubs, 8-40′
Nest Type: plate
Wingspan: 55″
Length: 32″

Though once decimated by nineteenth-century plume hunters seeking their ornate feathers which were used to adorn women's hats, the great egret population has rebounded to the point where they are difficult to miss in coastal habitats. They may often be observed standing motionless in water or stalking their aquatic prey before spearing it with a lightning-strike of their bill.

Great egrets, with their yellow bills and black feet, are easily distinguished from the smaller snowy egret which has a black bill and yellow feet. The plumage of a great egret is snow white, and they hold their necks in an "S" shape while flying and often while standing. Pure white plumage may seem to be a disadvantage in avoiding predators, but it is outweighed by the fact that the egrets' primary prey, fish, cannot readily discern them against the sky.

Snowy Egret

Egretta thula

Habitat: marsh, salt marsh, pond, tidal flats, estuaries
Food: aquatic invertebrates, fish, amphibians, reptiles
Nest Location: deciduous trees, shrubs, 5-10′
Nest Type: plate
Wingspan: 38″
Length: 20″

Snowy egrets were another near-victim of the nineteenth-century plume trade, their numbers decimated for the sake of their modified contour feathers, which were used for the frivolous decoration of hats. Thankfully, they have rebounded from the edge of extinction with a vengeance. Like their larger cousin, the great egret, snowy egrets are, as their name implies, snow white. They've also got a black bill, yellow spots in front of their eyes, black legs, and canary-yellow feet. During the breeding season, they develop elegant arching plumes on their backs, and at the height of their fervor the yellow feet and eye spots become infused with red.

Snowy egrets use their yellow feet to their advantage when feeding. Unlike the great egret and most others of their clan, the snowy egret actively pursues its prey rather than waiting patiently. Balanced steadily on one foot, it uses the other to probe the muddy bottom. If the disturbance doesn't startle its prey, the sight of that yellow foot flashing through the water does. The frog or fish that reacts to this will probably become the next course for the snowy egret.

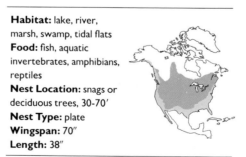

Great Blue Heron

Ardea herodias

Habitat: lake, river, marsh, swamp, tidal flats
Food: fish, aquatic invertebrates, amphibians, reptiles
Nest Location: snags or deciduous trees, 30-70′
Nest Type: plate
Wingspan: 70″
Length: 38″

Great blue herons are the largest and wariest wading birds of eastern North America; so wary, in fact, that many duck hunters use great blue heron decoys as a confidence lure to bring waterfowl in to their other decoys. With their height, super-sharp vision, and acute hearing, they are well equipped to serve as sentries of the marsh. Their departure at the first hint of danger signals other wildlife to be on the alert. Like many other large wading birds, great blue herons nest in colonies, called rookeries. This perhaps serves as a defense against predators.

With a relatively high ration of wing surface area to weight, great blue herons are remarkably strong fliers, cruising with their long legs trailing straight behind them and their neck curled in their typical "S" shaped position. The head is largely white with a slicked-back black crest and a yellow dagger-like bill. The back and wings are a bluish-gray color.

Green-backed Heron

Butorides striatus

Habitat: lake, pond, marsh, swamp, stream, tidal flats
Food: fish, aquatic invertebrates, terrestrial invertebrates, amphibians
Nest Location: deciduous trees & shrubs, 10-20′
Nest Type: plate
Wingspan: 25″
Length: 14″

The smallest and most common of our North American herons, the green-backed heron, is also undoubtedly the easiest one to approach, especially by non-motorized boat. Because of this and green-backed herons' tendency to remain motionless, canoeists and fishermen are often startled when the bird takes flight after they drift too close without seeing it.

In an interesting indication of birds' capacity for learning, a green-back heron was once observed placing scraps of bread it had found into the water and then feeding on the fish that came to nibble at the bread. Similar observation involving the use of baits as diverse as live insects, berries, twigs, and crackers have also been reported. Green-backed herons have even been seen pruning large twigs to smaller dimensions for this purpose, and so have engaged in tool manufacturing.

The green-backed heron, whose back and wings are actually more blue than green, is about crow-sized with a chestnut neck and cheeks, a small crest, and orange or greenish-yellow legs. The young are strong climbers.

Black-crowned Night Heron

Nycticorax nycticorax

Habitat: freshwater marsh, swamp, pond, salt marsh, tidal creek, estuary
Food: fish, aquatic invertebrates, amphibians
Nest Location: deciduous trees & shrubs, 15-30′
Nest Type: plate
Wingspan: 44″
Length: 20″

This species is somewhat stocky and short-necked compared with other herons. It sports a black crown which, during breeding season, has two or more long white plumes protruding rearward which it uses in courtship displays. Its bill and back are also black, its wings gray, underparts white, and legs pink or yellow. The long, splayed toes of wading birds support them well on the soft mud of their habitats.

True to their name, black-crowned night herons forage from dusk until dawn, roosting in trees by day. Their white underparts make it difficult for fish to see them against the sky. Like other herons, black-crowned night herons either wait motionlessly for their prey to approach them or stalk their prey with stealth and patience. They are colonial nesters, but are less inclined to nest in colonies of mixed species than are other herons.

ORDER GRUIFORMES, FAMILY GRUIDAE

Sandhill Crane

Grus canadensis

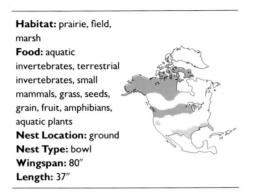

Habitat: prairie, field, marsh
Food: aquatic invertebrates, terrestrial invertebrates, small mammals, grass, seeds, grain, fruit, amphibians, aquatic plants
Nest Location: ground
Nest Type: bowl
Wingspan: 80″
Length: 37″

Tall, gray birds, sandhill cranes could be mistaken for great blue herons at a distance. Unlike great blue herons, which are solitary while foraging, sandhill cranes are normally seen in flocks and fly with their necks extended. Their crimson cap is bare skin that becomes infused with color during the breeding season.

Sandhill cranes migrate in huge flocks. They nest mostly in the Arctic, a fact that undoubtedly spared them the fate of their endangered relative, the whooping crane, whose population was reduced in 1941 to just 15 birds. Sandhill cranes, in fact, have played an important part in increasing the whooper population to its current level of more than 170. Both species normally lay 2 eggs as a safeguard against hatching failure, but if both hatch, the stronger chick ultimately will kill its weaker sibling. Sandhill cranes are conned into becoming foster parents by researchers who replace their own clutch with one whooping crane egg. The egg is readily accepted by the sandhill cranes, which virtually doubles the reproductive rate of whoopers by ensuring the survival of both their chicks.

ORDER GRUIFORMES, FAMILY RALLIDAE

Common Moorhen

Gallinula chloropus

Habitat: marsh, pond
Food: aquatic vegetation, aquatic invertebrates, terrestrial invertebrates, seeds, fruit
Nest Location: floating, ground, shrub
Nest Type: plate or cup
Wingspan: 21″
Length: 10.5″

Most members of the rail family are so secretive that few people ever see them. Fortunately, such is not the case with the common moorhen, not does it need extensive areas of marsh in which to forage and breed, as do most other rails. They are very easily recognized by their chickenlike profile, slate-gray head and breast, red bill and forehead, and yellow-green legs. White feathers under the tail and a constant head-bobbing motion are also clues. At close range, the yellow tip of the bill and red eyes are visible.

With diligent observation, the general behavior patterns of many animals become fairly predictable. Occasionally, however, Mother Nature throws us a curve ball just to keep our attention, or so it would seem. Among common moorhens, the female is larger than the male and does the courting, while the male dutifully assists in building nests and incubating the clutch. Incubation begins when the first egg is laid, meaning that there is a time lapse of up to two weeks between the first and last eggs hatching. The pair builds several nests on their territory, with the extras occupied by the female and youngsters at night while the male keeps incubating. The nests, wedged in dense reeds a foot or two above the water, are each equipped with ramps of reeds and cattails leading down to the water's surface.

American Coot

Fulica americana

Habitat: lake, pond, marsh, river
Food: aquatic vegetation, fish, aquatic invertebrates, terrestrial invertebrates
Nest Location: floating
Nest Type: plate
Wingspan: 25"
Length: 12"

Though duck-like in appearance and behavior, the American coot is a member of the rail family, composed primarily of secretive marsh birds. Its feet are lobed to aid in swimming, which it does with a back-and-forth pumping motion of its head, and it must sprint over the water to become airborne. American coots are plain birds, slate-gray with a black head and a conspicuous white, chicken-like bill. They are gregarious and prefer open water.

Throughout the bird world, there are many examples of totally different species associating with one another while feeding. In commensal associations, the activities of one species assist the foraging of another while neither deriving any benefits nor incurring any losses themselves. The "beaters", as they are called, stir up food which is also consumed by the "attendant" species. One of the classic examples of an attendant is the American coot, the panhandler of the bird world. Hopeful coots will feed in the wake of any of a number of other aquatic species, including redheads, canvasbacks, mallards, pintails, and tundra swans.

ORDER CHARADRIIFORMES,
FAMILY CHARADRIIDAE

Semipalmated Plover

Charadrius semipalmatus

Habitat: tidal flats, beaches
Food: aquatic invertebrates, terrestrial invertebrates, seeds
Nest Location: ground
Nest Type: scrape
Length: 5.75"

Those who are fond of long walks on the beach during the off-season have undoubtedly seen this bird. At first, the sand stretching ahead seems devoid of life, but as one continues, semipalmated plovers may begin to appear out of nowhere. At first, perhaps only one or two dash ahead, stopping periodically to assess the situation, but soon dozens may appear. Where did they come from?

It seems unlikely that one could miss a bird with such bold markings, yet these are their primary defense. Semipalmated plovers, along with killdeer and other banded plovers, exhibit what is known as disruptive coloration. The bold pattern of contrasting black and white markings disrupts their outline, visually breaking their body into disjunct pieces. When one looks at them without knowing they are there, the birds appear to be just bits of beach debris.

Semipalmated plovers are recognized by their short, orange, black-tipped bill, orange legs, dark back, white underparts, prominent black breast band, and bold facial pattern. Its name stems from the partial webbing between its toes, forming a partial "palm".

Killdeer

Charadrius vociferus

Habitat: meadow, grassland, tidal flats, suburban, urban
Food: terrestrial invertebrates
Nest Location: ground
Nest Type: scrape
Length: 8″

ORDER CHARADRIIFORMES,
FAMILY SCOLOPACIDAE

Long-billed Curlew

Numenius americanus

Habitat: grassland, meadow, salt marsh
Food: terrestrial invertebrates, aquatic invertebrates
Nest Location: ground
Nest Type: scrape
Length: 19″

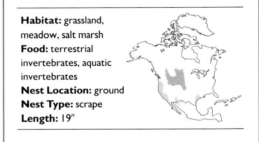

Willet

Catoptrophorus semipalmatus

Habitat: lake, marsh, salt marsh, tidal flats, beaches
Food: aquatic invertebrates
Nest Location: ground
Nest Type: scrape
Length: 13.5″

The killdeer is famous for its "broken wing" act. When approached too closely while on the nest, the parent feigns injury to its wing and darts ahead of the intruder with its attention-grabbing "killdeer" cry. Most of the time, the interloper falls for this ruse as the bird leads them far from the nest while staying just out of reach. When the nest seems safe, the killdeer will take flight, leaving its pursuer both surprised and frustrated.

Though they exhibit the same disruptive coloration as other banded plovers, which renders them unrecognizable when motionless, killdeer are the only ones with a rufous rump patch and *two* prominent breast bands. Their precocial chicks, looking like little puffballs on toothpick legs, have only one breast band, however. They prefer large expanses of short grass, and hence are often seen around airports, athletic fields, golf courses, pastures, and city parks.

In describing the long-billed curlew, one need scarcely mention anything after its ungainly, sickle-shaped mandibles. Despite the bill's awkward appearance, its owner can use it to obtain food located more than six inches deep in mud or sand, which it probes for crustaceans and worms. These birds are excellent examples of the diversity of bill-lengths that have evolved among shorebirds, which avoid competing for the same foods by probing at different depths in their muddy habitats.

Though reported to be common on the east coast until the mid-nineteenth century, it apparently succumbed to over-hunting there and is now adapted to summer life on the upland ranges of the West while wintering on the Gulf and southern Pacific coasts. It is mottled brown above with buff underparts and a cinnamon-colored lining under the wings.

The willet's black and white wing patches, called a flash pattern, can convey several messages. It is part of the bird's courtship and territorial displays, strengthening the pair bond and warning rival males away. In addition, the birds use their flashing wings to confuse and distract predators, diverting their attention from nearby eggs or nestlings. Close approach by an intruder will elicit the "broken wing" act characteristic of many ground-nesting shorebirds, and the bold wing pattern makes this performance even more effective. The flash pattern also serves as a cohesive signal that keeps the flock together in flight. The probability of becoming a predator's meal is quite a bit lower when in the midst of a group.

Aside from its wing pattern, the willet is a rather nondescript wading bird with a mottled grayish-brown plumage, which it molts after the breeding season, taking on an even blander appearance. It is most easily distinguished by its wing markings, bluish-gray legs, and a fairly heavy bill.

Spotted Sandpiper

Actitis macularia

Habitat: pond, lake, stream
Food: terrestrial invertebrates, aquatic invertebrates
Nest Location: ground
Nest Type: scrape
Length: 6.25″

Unlike most other shorebirds, spotted sandpipers prefer to breed near inland bodies of fresh water, where they feed largely on flying insects but will also take crustaceans, mollusks, fish, and worms.

This is one species that bucks tradition. The female arrives first on the breeding grounds, displays to attract males, and defends a large territory encompassing the smaller territories of its mates. The female produces up to five clutches of eggs, each one fertilized by a different male, who in turn incubates the eggs and raises the young. The spotted sandpiper uses this unusual breeding arrangement, which is known as polyandry, to take advantage of the long nesting season of the temperate latitudes and produce more offspring, which is the mark of evolutionary success among living organisms.

True to its name, the spotted sandpiper in summer plumage has a white breast evenly marked with dark round spots. It is most easily identified by its characteristic stance with its body tilted forward, head held low, and tail continuously bobbing up and down. Their flight is also diagnostic: short bursts of rapid, shallow wing beats interspersed with short glides.

Dunlin

Calidris alpina

Habitat: beach, tidal flats
Food: terrestrial invertebrates, aquatic invertebrates
Nest Location: ground
Nest Type: scrape
Length: 7″

"All things hiddenly connected are, so that we can't disturb a flower without the troubling of a star." I don't remember the source of that paraphrased quote, but it has stuck with me for many years. It sums up perfectly an important aspect of the dunlin's life cycle. Dunlin, like many other shorebirds, spend the winter far south of their breeding grounds. Recent studies have revealed that these migrants time their journeys so that their arrival at a certain few critical locations, called staging areas, coincides with brief but super-abundant food sources that allow them to quickly replenish their energy reserves and be on their way. A perfect example of this phenomenon is the annual arrival and departure of up to 1.5 million shorebirds in concentrated areas along the Delaware Bay coinciding with the egg-laying of the Bay's horseshoe crabs. If these few areas are not protected, even abundant species like the dunlin could be in serious jeopardy.

Should you spot them during their spring migration, you will recognize dunlin by their rusty backs, white underparts, and a large black patch on their bellies. Their perfectly synchronized flight in tight formation is characterized by alternate flashes of white and brown as the flock turns in unison.

Sanderling

Calidris alba

Habitat: coastal beaches

Food: terrestrial invertebrates, aquatic invertebrates

Nest Location: ground

Nest Type: scrape

Length: 6.5"

One of the more common sights on sandy seaside beaches are flocks of small birds rhythmically chasing each retreating wave down the sloping sands and then withdrawing to escape the frothy advance of the next, like so many mechanical toys. At first, their antics may seem like a game of "chicken" to see which can linger the longest before an incoming wave without getting its feet wet. Careful observation soon reveals, however, that these nimble birds are engaged in the very serious game of survival.

Each wave washes up countless tiny mollusks, crustaceans, and worms from deeper water onto the beach. Before the froth has completely subsided, these creatures are frantically burrowing back into the sand. Just as quickly, sanderlings are there to snatch them up hence their ritual running to and from the water's edge. Were they not so badly outnumbered, these voracious little "peeps", as shorebirds are generically called, might pose a serious threat to their prey populations.

In summer plumage, sanderlings are rusty on their head, neck, and breast, with white underparts. By the time they have returned in late summer from their breeding grounds on the arctic tundra, they have molted to a light gray above to become the palest of sandpipers. Flocks fly in tight, synchronous formation with each bird emanating high pitched calls to help them avoid mid-air collisions. In flight, the broad, white wing stripe lengthwise on their dark wing is diagnostic.

American Woodcock

Philohela minor

Habitat: swamp, thicket, meadow, deciduous forest

Food: terrestrial invertebrates

Nest Location: ground

Nest Type: scrape

Length: 8.25"

Also known as a timberdoodle, the American woodcock is a strange bird indeed! Though it is a member of the sandpiper family, this upland game bird prefers to make its home in wooded areas. With its stocky body and stubby wings, it hardly looks like it could even get airborne, but the woodcock is actually a fair flier that undertakes a migration of hundreds of miles every spring and fall. With its masterful camouflage, the woodcock will permit your close approach, gambling that you will not see it. Take one step too near, however, and it bursts forth in a startling flurry of

wing beats, sometimes literally from underfoot. It is a challenging quarry for sportsmen, for it presents a very difficult target with its small size and zigzagging flight through the trees and brush.

The woodcock's bulging eyes are positioned high on its head, affording a 360 degree view that effectively prevents surprise attacks by predators. Its rounded wings are attached to a rotund body having rufous underparts and a brown speckled back that blends perfectly with the dead leaves on the floor of a thicket or deciduous forest. Perhaps its bill is most noteworthy, not so much for its size but for the ability of the sensitive upper mandible to hinge open at the tip, a trait which enables woodcocks to probe deep in the soil and seize their favorite food, earthworms.

Among other naturalists in eastern North America, it is a spring ritual to go out into a brushy meadow or pasture at dusk to watch and hear the courtship and territorial flight-displays of male woodcocks over their breeding grounds. On the ground, the male

patrols his territory, rendering a nasal "peent" every few seconds. He then takes off, circling over his territory in an upward spiral, a twittering sound created as air rushes through specialized, stiff outer wing feathers. At the zenith, he tumbles earthward, a burst of bubbling notes emanating from his modified flight feathers. Finally, he swoops in to a landing, often within a few feet of the takeoff point, and resumes "peenting".

Greater Yellowlegs

Tringa melanoleuca

Habitat: marsh, tidal
flats, stream, pond, bogs
Food: fish, aquatic
invertebrates
Nest Location: ground
Nest Type: scrape
Length: 11″

Yellowlegs take flight easily when alarmed, their vocal departure and flashing white rump patch warning other animals of possible danger, hence their old nickname, "telltales". They nest on the tundra and muskeg of the far north, but are common in the United States while wintering in coastal areas and during migration.

The long legs of this bird enable it to wade into deeper water than can most small shorebirds, where, instead of probing mud with its slightly upturned bill, it sweeps the water for small fish and invertebrates. It is nearly identical to the lesser yellowlegs except for its larger size and stouter bill; both are slim with a flecked pattern of white, black, and gray.

Common Snipe

Gallinago gallinago

Habitat: freshwater
marsh, pond, bog,
meadow
Food: terrestrial
invertebrates, aquatic
invertebrates
Nest Location: ground
Nest Type: scrape
Length: 9″

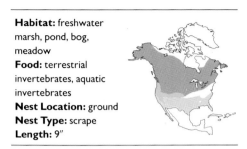

A common prank among children while camping is to send someone on a "snipe hunt", a fruitless pursuit of a mythical creature that is meant to humiliate gullible campers. In fact, the snipe is as real as you or I. It is another member of the sandpiper family, closely related to American woodcock. Like the woodcock, the male snipe performs an impressive courtship flight. Air passing through his parted, rigid tail feathers produces a pulsating hum during his swooping descent.

Snipe look more like sandpipers than do woodcock. They have a brownish, heavily streaked head and a long bill. When flushe, they utter a grating call and fly on a zigzag course, revealing the short orangish tail.

ORDER CHARADRIIFORMES,
FAMILY LARIDAE

Herring Gull

Larus argentatus

Habitat: beach, salt
marsh, tidal flats, lake,
river, estuary, field
Food: nearly anything,
most scavenger
Nest Location: ground,
cliff
Nest Type: bowl
Wingspan: 55″
Length: 20″

Few birds capture the grace of flight so well as gulls, of which herring gulls are our most abundant species. A scavenger without standards, the herring gull will eat literally anything it can digest. Garbage dumps associated with the large human populatio near the coasts are responsible for the boom in herring gull populations. They are noted for their habit of dropping shellfish from a height onto rocks or pavement in order to break them open so they can reach the soft tissue inside.

Herring gulls are white birds, with gray across the wings and back and black wing tips. Other field marks include pink legs and a yellow bill with a large red spot on the tip of the lower mandible. This red spot, when pecked by the young gulls, triggers a regurgitation reflex, which is how the parents deliver food to their offspring.

Ring-billed Gull

Larus delawarensis

Habitat: lake, river, field, beach, estuaries
Food: fish, terrestrial invertebrates, small mammals, scavenger
Nest Location: ground
Nest Type: bowl
Wingspan: 49″
Length: 16″

Ring-billed gull

Our most common inland gull is the ring-billed gull, dubbed by noted nineteenth-century naturalist and artist John James Audubon as "the great American gull". Frequently found on lakes and larger rivers, they are also not uncommon near salt water habitats. They are voracious insect-eaters and can often be seen in large flocks swarming after tractors in farm fields, feasting on grasshoppers and other invertebrates stirred up by the farmer. They nest in huge colonies on isolated islands; more than 85,000 pairs were counted on one Lake Ontario island alone.

With such potential for confusion among colonial parents as to whose chick belongs to whom, it is imperative that they learn to recognize their own offspring, especially for species in which the chicks will leave the nest while still dependent upon their parents. This ensures that they do not waste energy caring for another's young while neglecting their own. Studies have shown that ring-billed gulls are somehow able to distinguish their offspring by sight, which is unlike other species in similar circumstances that are dependent upon voice recognition.

Adult ring-billed gulls differ from the slightly larger herring gulls in their yellow legs and the distinctive black ring encircling their yellow bill. Excepting these traits, they are otherwise very similar, having a gray back and wings, black wing tips, and otherwise white plumage.

Laughing gulls

Laughing Gull

Larus atricillia

Habitat: salt marsh, beach, estuaries
Food: aquatic invertebrates, fish, terrestrial invertebrates
Nest Location: ground
Nest Type: scrape
Wingspan: 41″
Length: 13″

One of the most typical sounds along the eastern seaboard and the Gulf Coast is the maniacal laughter of the laughing gull, sounding like some crazed soul chortling with glee. They are seldom found far from salt water, although they sometimes visit coastal farmlands to feed on insects and earthworms in freshly-plowed fields. They consume large numbers of biting green-headed flies, the bane of coastal residents and visitors.

It is not lost upon laughing gulls that an easy meal can be had from pelicans. When these opportunists witness a pelican making a catch, they perch on the big bird's head with hopes of snatching a fish from the pelican when it opens its bill to shift the fish into a better position for swallowing.

These birds nest in colonies, usually in the tall beach grass or in salt marshes. Like many colonial nesters, they must learn to recognize their own offspring in order to ensure their survival. Unlike ring-billed gulls which identify their own young by sight, laughing gulls distinguish their chicks by the young birds' response to their calls.

In summer plumage, laughing gulls possess a black hood, a deep red bill, and dark gray wings blending into black wing tips. Upon molting into their winter plumage, however, they lose the black hood and replace it with a gray smudge on the back of their white head; the bill also loses its red color.

Royal Tern

Sterna maxima

Habitat: beach
Food: fish, aquatic invertebrates
Nest Location: ground
Nest Type: scrape
Wingspan: 43″
Length: 18″

Though very common along the Atlantic and Gulf coasts, the royal tern does not stray from salt water. They nest in very dense colonies on deserted beaches and isolated sand bars, with each territory providing just enough room for a parent to incubate its single egg. After leaving the nest but before they can fly, fledglings congregate in a group called a creche, which is supervised by a few adult guardians. Though it is unusual among wild animals to care for the offspring of others, this practice benefits royal terns by freeing the parents to do more foraging, so they are better able to feed both themselves and their growing dependents. They are also able to mount a mass attack upon a predator and drive it away while the young birds are herded to safety by their caretakers.

The royal tern shares traits common to a number of other terns, such as a slender build and long, pointed wings, mostly-white plumage, light gray wings and back, and a black crest. Its white forehead is briefly replaced by a solid black cap during the breeding season. It is larger than all other eastern terns except the caspian tern, from which it can be told by its white forehead and thick, orange bill as opposed to the blood-red bill of the caspian.

ORDER COLUMBIFORMES,
FAMILY COLUMBIDAE

Mourning Dove

Zenaida macroura

Habitat: field, prairie, thicket, forest edge, urban
Food: seeds, grain
Nest Location: deciduous tree, coniferous tree, 0-40′, ground
Nest Type: plate
Length: 10.5″

Each fall, many shotgun shells are spent in vain on this feathered jet. They are among the fastest of game birds, and with their small size they present an extremely challenging target, so one needn't fret for the mourning dove population. Their species has actually benefited from the clearing of North American forests, having increased greatly with the spread of agriculture.

The plaintive call of the mourning dove heard throughout much of North America in the spring is actually a courtship and territorial call marking their season of renewal. Their nest is no engineering marvel, being little more than a bunch of twigs wedged precariously in the crotch of a branch. So flimsy is this structure that the panicked departure of a frightened dove on whistling wings is sometimes enough to dislodge an egg from its haven. Judging from the abundance of this species, however, accidents such as these are apparently not much of a problem for it.

Adults feed their nestling a regurgitated food called "pigeon milk", a substance rich in protein and fat which is secreted by glands in the parents' crop. The crop is a storage organ located near the beginning of a bird's digestive tract that allows it to eat quickly, while it is often vulnerable, and store and soften the food until the stomach can accommodate it. Some species lack crops, among them owls and many sea bird which rely solely on their glandular stomach to dissolve the edible portions of their prey.

ORDER STRIGIFORMES, FAMILY STRIGIDAE

Eastern Screech Owl

Otus asio

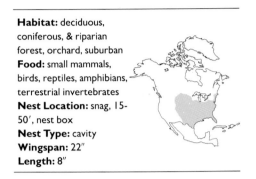

Habitat: deciduous, coniferous, & riparian forest, orchard, suburban
Food: small mammals, birds, reptiles, amphibians, terrestrial invertebrates
Nest Location: snag, 15-50′, nest box
Nest Type: cavity
Wingspan: 22″
Length: 8″

Setting screech owls apart from the rest of North American birds is their characteristic of having two distinct color phases that have nothing to do with sex, age, or season. The gray phase is the "normal" color, while the red phase is caused by excessive red pigment, a condition known as erythrism. It is not unusual for the same brood of nestlings to include both red phase and gray phase individuals. Adults have heavily streaked breasts, and yellow eyes. This is the only small eastern owl with ear tufts.

Screech owls have been known to take prey as large as rats and ruffed grouse, but they generally prefer smaller fare, and are even reputed to occasionally take small fish and crayfish from streams. Since they hunt mostly at night, they, like many other owls, depend heavily upon their sense of hearing for success. The "ears" they appear to have, though, are really just tufts of feathers. Their real ears are located on the sides of the head and are asymmetrical so that the bird can differentiate sounds originating from above, below, left, and right.

Great Horned Owl

Bubo virginianus

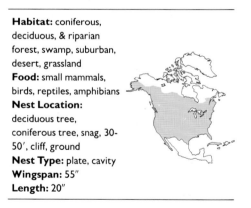

Habitat: coniferous, deciduous, & riparian forest, swamp, suburban, desert, grassland
Food: small mammals, birds, reptiles, amphibians
Nest Location: deciduous tree, coniferous tree, snag, 30-50′, cliff, ground
Nest Type: plate, cavity
Wingspan: 55″
Length: 20″

It isn't called the flying tiger for nothing. The great horned owl is a fierce bird of prey, armed with deadly talons that can dispatch prey as formidable as porcupines, and not afraid of a fight. The first primary feather on each wing is saw-toothed, rather than smooth, to disrupt air flow over the smooth wing surface and totally eliminate the sound it would normally cause, allowing this bird to descend on its prey in total silence. The fine horizontal bars on their breasts and bellies distinguish great horned owls from their smaller look-alikes, long-eared owls, which are streaked vertically in the same area.

Perfect for tearing bite-sized chunks of flesh from larger victims, the strong and sharp hooked beak of this raptor is characteristic of birds of prey. Because they swallow smaller prey whole and have no teeth to chew with, raptors like the great horned owl ingest material that their digestive systems cannot handle, such as bones, hair, and feathers. For their own well-being, they must periodically regurgitate this material in felt-like wads called pellets, usually one per victim. Despite their unsavory appearance, pellets are fairly sanitary, and a curious naturalist can learn a great deal about these birds by dissecting their pellets in order to identify their latest meals.

Great horned owls prefer to use abandoned hawk or eagle nests, and rarely do they build their own. The hardy soul who ventures outside on January evenings stands a very good chance of hearing the courtship calls of these birds.

Long-eared Owl

Asio otus

Habitat: coniferous, mixed, riparian forest, orchard
Food: small mammals, birds, terrestrial invertebrates
Nest Location: deciduous tree, 25-35', snag, ground
Nest Type: plate, cavity, scrape
Wingspan: 41"
Length: 13"

Long-eared owls are well-named, but like other "eared" owls, these tufts of feathers have nothing to do with hearing. More functional in this capacity is the chestnut-colored ruff of feathers known as a facial disk. The facial disk channels sound to the large ear openings hidden on the sides of the head, serving to amplify the sound waves for an already acute sense of hearing. The ear openings are asymmetrical in size, shape, and position, enabling the bird to pinpoint sounds with accuracy.

Long-eared owls are smaller and more slender than the similar great horned owl, but they may appear larger in flight. They also prefer to use abandoned nests of other large birds, or even those of squirrels. Their typical haunt is in conifer stands. When trying to avoid detection by humans or other interlopers, long-eared owls do a quite convincing impression of a broken branch by sitting very erect and compressing their feathers to appear slimmer.

Barred Owl

Strix varia

Habitat: coniferous, mixed, and riparian forest, swamp
Food: small mammals, birds, amphibians, reptiles
Nest Location: snag, 20-50'
Nest Type: cavity
Wingspan: 44"
Length: 17"

Barred owls have a combination of fine, brown, horizontal bars on their throat and upper breast (hence their name) and vertical brown streaks on their lower breast and belly. Unlike most other owls, which have yellow eyes, those of barred owls are large and brown, contributing to their cuddly teddy bear appearance. Their extra large pupils and the retinas of their eyes, packed with light-sensitive cells called rods, afford excellent low-light vision. This, combined with their superior sense of hearing, enables them to hunt primarily at night, but they may also be active during the day. It is a myth that owls can see in total darkness and that they cannot see in daylight.

Though it has a wide range of vocalizations, the typical call of a barred owl is higher pitched than the bass hoot of a great horned owl and is made to the cadence of "Who cooks for you, who cooks for you-all?" One of these two species is usually what is referred to by the term "hoot owl".

Burrowing Owl

Athene cunicularia

Habitat: grassland, savanna, desert, field, suburban
Food: small mammals, birds, reptiles, terrestrial invertebrates
Nest Location: underground
Nest Type: burrow
Wingspan: 22"
Length: 8"

Owls are unabashed opportunists when it comes to nesting, but the burrowing owl takes this trait to an extreme level. While many owls prefer to use tree cavities or to commandeer the deserted nest of some large bird or squirrel, burrowing owls have taken the low road, literally. Over the millennia they have developed an affinity for burrows, mostly those abandoned by prairie dogs, squirrels, or other rodents, although they are capable of digging their own.

Burrowing owls are diurnal, or active by day, further bucking tradition. Their glaring yellow eyes, arching eyebrows, and long legs combine to lend the bird a comical air like that of some frustrated cartoon character. In the open expanses they inhabit, these owls may be seen perched atop fenceposts or other vantage points to survey their surroundings. Their faces are framed by a dark collar around the neck, and light spots adorn their upper breast and back, a pattern that reverses itself on the belly.

Short-eared Owl

Asio flammeus

Habitat: grassland, field, marsh, salt marsh
Food: small mammals, birds, terrestrial invertebrates
Nest Location: ground
Nest Type: scrape
Wingspan: 41″
Length: 13″

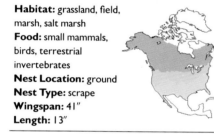

Owls have a reputation as denizens of the night, but the short-eared owl is often seen as it begins hunting in the late afternoon. With an affinity for open country, this is probably the owl seen most often in North America. It has an erratic, fluttering flight and hovers frequently as it searches the grass for rodents.

The ear tufts of these owls are indeed short; in fact they are barely visible even at close range. Their penetrating yellow eyes are set in dark patches on their facial disk, the ruff of feathers that funnels sound to their hidden ears. A heavily streaked, tawny-brown breast and noticeably long wings complete their physical description.

Short-eared owls have possibly the largest range in North America, and they are reportedly found on every other continent as well. World-wide, they are important elements in the control of rodent populations.

ORDER CAPRIMULGIFORMES, FAMILY CAPRIMULGIDAE

Common Nighthawk

Chordeiles minor

Habitat: urban, suburban, fields, savanna, grassland
Food: terrestrial invertebrates
Nest Location: ground, buildings
Nest Type: none
Wingspan: 23″
Length: 9″

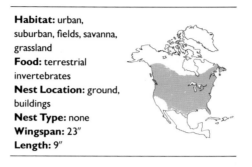

Common nighthawks suffer the indignity of having been misnamed at least four times. They are not strictly nocturnal, nor are they hawks at all, but belong to a group of birds commonly called goatsuckers, a colorful name derived from European folklore that conjures up bizarre images in the mind. A similar bird of Europe, the nightjar, exhibited a preference for pastures and other open places often frequented by livestock. Observant individuals noticed this and concluded that the nightjars must have been drawn to the animals, and that perhaps they sucked milk from these animals on their nightly sojourns. The bird is also known in some parts as a bull bat, in reference to sounds made by its feathers during courtship flights, but clearly this is no bat either.

Appearances are misleading with the nighthawk. At first glance, it seems to possess a bill so tiny that one wonders what it could possibly consume. Upon closer scrutiny, though, it is evident that its mouth extends far back along the sides of its head and can open to reveal a cavernous orifice, perfect for scooping up flying insects on the wing as the nighthawk does. A white throat patch, and white bars on the stream-lined wings of this dark bird, are sufficient field marks for identification.

Nighthawks make no nest at all, but simply lay their egg in what they deem a suitable spot. They once nested on dry river beds and gravel bars, but have adapted easily to the flat rooftops of city buildings with the advent of civilization. Over the breeding grounds, the male interrupts his foraging flights to perform power dives over and over again. When he pulls out, the air rushing through his wing feathers produces what has been referred to as a booming sound but is more accurately described as a musical hum.

ORDER APODIFORMES,
FAMILY TROCHILIDAE

Ruby-throated Hummingbird

Archilochus colubris

Habitat: suburban, deciduous and mixed forest, forest edge
Food: nectar, terrestrial invertebrates, tree sap
Nest Location: deciduous tree, 10-20′
Nest Type: cup
Length: 3″

Ornithologists have long known that ruby-throated hummingbirds returned north from their winter range in Mexico and Central America well before many flowers were in bloom, but how they survived this period remained a mystery for some time. Today we know that these feathered jewels have enterprisingly adopted a commensal feeding relationship with yellow-bellied sapsuckers, a species of woodpecker. The hummers, as "attendants", follow sapsuckers as they drill horizontal rows of "wells" in living trees in order to harvest the sap. These wells become the source of food for hummingbirds, as well, who partake of the sugary sap as well as the protein-rich insects it attracts.

Hummingbirds will readily accept a sugar water solution from a feeder or even from a bowl, although the latter method is sure to draw many ants as well. Care must be taken to mix the sugar water in the proper concentration, however, for a solution too strong or too weak will kill them. Hummers find the color red to be extremely attractive, so tie a red ribbon on your feeder or choose one with red parts. Avoid using red food dyes in their food, though; they don't need it, and it could be harmful to them.

Ruby-throated hummingbirds draw their name from the jewel-like throat patch of the male that flashes a brilliant scarlet in sunlight. Both sexes are emerald-green above with whitish underparts. So aerodynamically adept are hummingbirds that they have completely lost the ability to walk. Their weak feet and legs serve only to grip perches.

Costa's Hummingbird

Calypte costae

Habitat: desert, suburban
Food: nectar, terrestrial invertebrates
Nest Location: shrub, deciduous tree, 3-5′
Nest Type: cup
Length: 3″

Though their range is not large, Costa's hummingbirds are common in their southwestern desert habitat. Among North American hummingbirds, the violet throat flanked by long side feathers and the violet cap combined with a green back and flanks are identifying features of a male Costa's hummingbird. Females, with metallic green backs, pale breasts, and white-tipped black tails, resemble those of several other species. The tail feathers of males produce a metallic sound during courtship flights.

Viewed from certain angles, male Costa's hummers may seem unimpressive, but they seem to know exactly the right angles that will send amethyst flashes toward their prospective mates during courtship. Like the iridescent plumage of any other bird, that of hummingbirds is due to the microscopic structure of the feathers which reflect light with a prismatic effect, resulting in flashes of color. When one sees these feathered jewels glinting in the sunlight, it becomes evident why Aztec leaders used their skins on ceremonial robes to invoke an air of divinity.

Rufous Hummingbird

Selasphorus rufus

Habitat: coniferous forest, thickets, meadows
Food: nectar, terrestrial invertebrates
Nest Location: conifers, deciduous trees, 1-15'
Nest Type: cup
Length: 3.5"

In addition to securing their own nest site, rufous hummingbirds also claim and zealously defend feeding territories high in the wildflower-spangled meadows of the Rocky Mountains and the Cascade Range of the Pacific Northwest. In a unique twist, they also establish feeding territories during migration that serve as their own private refuelling stop.

Since they are in constant competition with other nectar feeders, rufous hummingbirds have perfected a feeding strategy that gets them the best return on their energy investment. Beginning first thing in the morning, they patrol the perimeter of their little empire, feasting on nectar while evicting trespassing bees, butterflies, hawkmoths, and other hummers. Throughout the day, the path of this coppery dynamo spirals systematically inward, so that any competitors trying to sneak a drink at the edge of its domain are likely to find only flowers already depleted of nectar.

The migration of rufous hummingbirds takes them on a looping tour of the western mountains. In late winter they begin their journey north along the Pacific coast, taking advantage of the mild climate there. By July they have already reached their breeding territory, raised a brood of young birds, and are now on a southeasterly route just in time to take advantage of the "spring" wildflowers in the alpine meadows of the central Rockies.

Males are non-iridescent rufous on their back and sides, white on the breast, and are endowed with a radiant orangish-red throat patch. Female rufous hummers are green above with a touch of rufous on their sides and at the base of their tail.

ORDER CORACIIFORMES,
FAMILY ALCEDINIDAE

Belted Kingfisher

Ceryle alcyon

Habitat: stream, river, lake, pond, coastal
Food: fish, amphibians, reptiles
Nest Location: underground
Nest Type: burrow
Length: 12"

You're canoeing along the shore or a peaceful lake in the summer. You cease paddling and drift along, slipping deeper into a daydream appropriate to the restful atmosphere when – Splash! Jolted rudely back to reality, you turn about just in time to see a belted kingfisher making off with the next course of his lunch.

Kingfishers are frequently seen chattering raucously on an undulating flight to their next perch or hovering high over the water just before entering into a kamikaze-style dive after their next victim. Ravenous fish eaters, they will also take salamanders, newts, frogs, lizards, insects, and even crabs.

Most striking about a belted kingfisher's appearance is its unusually large head, almost comical in relation to the rest of the body. They are bluish-gray on the head, breast, and back, with a ragged crest, a white collar, and a white belly. Females have a rusty band across their belly which the males lack.

During the nesting season, home is a burrow excavated by the kingfishers themselves. Using their bills, they chisel a tunnel as much as eight feet into an earthen bank near their fishing grounds, kicking the debris toward the burrow entrance. The burrow culminates in a nesting chamber where the eggs are laid and incubated. Both parents share the incubating chore, but the female alone broods the nestlings for the first few days after they hatch while her mate feeds the whole family.

ORDER PICIFORMES, FAMILY PICIDAE

Northern Flicker

Colaptes auratus

Habitat: deciduous, coniferous, and mixed forest, fields, suburban
Food: terrestrial invertebrates
Nest Location: snag, 6-15′, nest box
Nest Type: cavity
Length: 10.5″

Though they belong to the same family, flickers have deviated from typical woodpecker behavior. They nest in tree cavities like other woodpeckers, but whereas most of their kin feed on insects found in dead wood, northern flickers satisfy their tastes with ground-level fare. They will sample fallen fruits, seeds, nuts, and various insects, but their real weakness is ants, which they consume in copious quantities. Their diminished reliance on snags and a fondness for clearings where their food is more easily found have allowed this species to adapt to civilization better than any other woodpecker. They are especially common around farmland, forest edges, suburban areas, and city parks.

The northern flicker is something of an anomaly for birdwatchers, because it includes what were considered, until recently, three distinct species. Among these three, formerly the yellow-shafted, red-shafted, and gilded flickers, there have apparently been instances of successful interbreeding, leading ornithological authorities to lump them into a single species. All have a light breast with black spots, a black crescent breast band, and a bold white rump patch, but there the similarities end. The eastern race is identified by the combination of bright yellow under the wings, a tan face, a gray cap, and a red crescent on the nape of the neck. In contrast, members of the western race are colored red under their wings, and have a gray face and tan cap. The same gray face and tan cap mark the southwestern species, but their wings are yellow underneath. Eastern males sport a black "mustache" mark, while the mustache of western males is red. Confused? You should be.

Red-bellied Woodpecker

Melanerpes carolinus

Habitat: deciduous and riparian forest, swamp, suburban
Food: terrestrial invertebrates, nuts, fruit, seeds
Nest Location: snag, 5-40′
Nest Type: cavity
Length: 8.5″

Red-bellied woodpecker is a misnomer, for there is really very little red on their bellies, just a hint of orange. The black and white bars running from wing to wing across the back of this and similar species have earned them the nicknames "ladder-backed" and "zebra-backed" woodpeckers. Both sexes have a red nape, but only the male has a red cap as well, while the female sports a gray cap.

Like other woodpeckers, red-bellied woodpeckers have acquired some specialized features as they evolved into their present lifestyles. One of these is the rigid and pointed tail feathers that they use very effectively as a prop when climbing or resting on tree trunks. Another is the toe arrangement; most birds have three toes pointing forward and one backward, but woodpeckers are well-adapted for gripping vertical tree bark with two toes forward and two backward. Together, the tail and feet form a very strong tripod from which the woodpecker can pound away as it chisels a nest cavity or a hole in search of food.

Yellow-bellied Sapsucker

Sphyrapicus varius

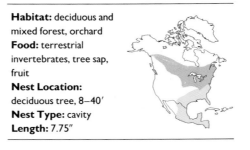

Habitat: deciduous and mixed forest, orchard
Food: terrestrial invertebrates, tree sap, fruit
Nest Location: deciduous tree, 8–40'
Nest Type: cavity
Length: 7.75"

In contrast to the red-bellied woodpecker, the yellow-bellied sapsucker's name, even though comical, is quite appropriate. Its belly is yellowish and it does, in fact, eat tree sap, which it collects from horizontal rows of wells it drills in living trees, especially apple trees. It also feeds extensively on insects and berries.

It's hard to say whether sapsuckers' habit of drilling for sap evolved as a means of attracting insects, or if their objective is really the sweet sap and insects attracted to it are merely a bonus. In any case, their specialized tongue is undoubtedly a clue. Unlike other woodpeckers, who possess extremely long, barbed tongues adapted to reaching deep into narrow cavities and seizing insects, the yellow-bellied sapsucker has a comparatively short tongue covered with fine hairs, so it is unable to feed in conventional woodpecker fashion.

In additiion to their yellow-tinged bellies, yellow-bellied sapsuckers exhibit a black-and-white striped face, a red forehead, and conspicuous white wing patches. Males have red throats, while those of females are white.

Downy Woodpecker

Picoides pubescens

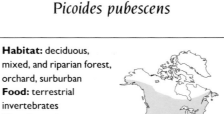

Habitat: deciduous, mixed, and riparian forest, orchard, surburban
Food: terrestrial invertebrates
Nest Location: snag, 3–50'
Nest Type: cavity
Length: 5.75"

Our smallest North American woodpecker, the down woodpecker is also the most common and widespread of its clan, absent only in the relatively treeless deserts and grassland of the Southwest. This species is rather simply marked with a white breast, a white stripe down the middle of the black back, a black-and-white striped face, and a black cap. Males have a red patch on the back of their head. Their scruffy appearance about the bill results from the dense bristles covering their nostrils and protecting their lungs from the dust they raise while pecking. Except for their size, about 50 per cent larger than the downy, hairy woodpeckers are nearly identical to them in appearance, habitat, and behavior.

In lieu of song, the downy and other woodpeckers use drumming, a rapid-fire tapping on wood or other resonant surfaces, as part of their courtship and in asserting their dominance over a particular piece of real estate. With practice, different species can be distinguished by the tempo, length, and volume of their drumming. Flickers, for example, like to drum on metal, and have been observed pounding on flagpoles, heavy machinery, and metal roofs. A slower tapping is used by mated pairs to converse with each other. Woodpeckers supplement these non-vocal communications with a variety of calls.

Woodpeckers form their nests in the cavities of trees.

ORDER PASSERIFORMES, FAMILY TYRANNIDAE

Eastern Kingbird

Tyrannus tyrannus

Habitat: forest edge, riparian forest, field, orchard
Food: terrestrial invertebrates, fruit
Nest Location: deciduous trees, shrubs, 8–25'
Nest Type: cup
Length: 6.75"

With a Latin name that translates to "tyrant of tyrants", one can expect aggressive behavior from the eastern kingbird, and that's exactly what we see in this fiercely territorial bird. From an exposed perch it utters its rasping, staccato call, launching into a raging tirade and driving intruders from its domain when they are careless enough or bold enough to enter. The clamor rallies nearby small birds which join in "mobbing" larger predators like hawks. The effect of mobbing, numbers of smaller birds swarming noisily around their enemy, is to frustrate the predator, telling it that the element of surprise has been lost and that it is fruitless to remain. The kingbird spearheads the assault and does not accept victory until its foe is in full retreat.

With its solid black hood pulled down over its eyes, the eastern kingbird looks more like the royal executioner than the king. It is easily recognized by the solid black back, wings, and tail, contrasting white underparts, and a terminal white band on its tail. They sometimes flash a bright red patch on their crown, but it normally remains hidden beneath contour feathers. In typical flycatcher feeding behavior, it darts from an exposed perch to snatch flying insects on the wing and return to the same or a nearby perch.

Eastern Phoebe

Sayornis phoebe

Habitat: stream, pond, riparian forest, farm, suburban
Food: terrestrial invertebrates
Nest Location: building, bridge, cliff
Nest Type: cup
Length: 5.75"

As a certain but little-known sign of spring, the eastern phoebe announces its arrival, insistently calling its name over and over while diligently pumping its tail down and up for emphasis. This is a very nondescript bird, with no prominent field marks, but the tail pumping and constant "fee-bee" call are sufficient to identify it.

Before the settlement of this continent, eastern phoebes nested on cliffs and rock overhangs, especially near water. They seem to have found civilization very much

to their liking, as they now nest most frequently on man-made structures like bridges, eaves, and porches, and other sheltered sites. The nest, made of mud, moss, plant fibers, and sometimes hair, is firmly anchored to its site. On the nest, the female is quite tame, permitting human approach to within several feet before she flees to a nearby perch to watch nervously.

Like other members of the insectivorous flycatcher family, eastern phoebes feed by hawking insects. From their vantage point on an exposed perch, the birds dart out when they spy a flying insect, pick it off in mid-air, and return, often to the same perch or one very close by.

Great Crested Flycatcher

Myiarchus crinitus

Habitat: forest edge, deciduous woodland, orchard
Food: terrestrial invertebrates, fruit
Nest Location: deciduous tree, snag, 10–50'
Nest Type: cavity
Length: 7"

This is the forest counterpart of the eastern kingbird. The grating "Wheeeep?" call is heard much more often than this bird is seen, however, for it spends much time in the forest canopy hawking insects and patrolling its territory. Its crest is not very pronounced, even though the name implies it would be. Olive-brown on the head and neck gradually grades into reddish-brown on the wings and tail. The throat and breast are gray, while the belly and flanks are a pleasing pastel yellow.

Much has been made of the fact that great crested flycatchers like to incorporate shed snake skins in their nest linings. Folklore has it that the bird does this in order to intimidate potential predators. More than likely, they have simply developed an affinity for the texture and workability of snake skins, for they will also use similar artificial materials like waxed paper, cellophane, and plastic when available.

Willow Flycatcher

Empidonax traillii

Habitat: swamp, thicket
Food: terrestrial invertebrates, fruit
Nest Location: shrub, deciduous tree, 2–10'
Nest Type: cup
Length: 4.75"

Dusky, olive-gray flycatchers, especially those of the genus *Empidonax sp.*, are extremely difficult to identify, even for veteran birders. They have very few field marks, similar coloration, and are most readily differentiated by song, even among themselves. Strikingly similar species that are nonetheless reproductively autonomous (do not interbreed) are considered by scientists to be "sibling species". They are really examples of evolution in action, descendants of a single species that, through the process of natural selection, have responded to environmental pressures differently. How rapidly they drift apart depends upon the severity of these pressures.

Willow flycatchers and alder flycatchers are perfect examples of this. With olive-brown backs, white throats, and two pale

wing bars, they are virtually identical except for slight variations in song. Despite this, they mate only within their own species. The different species show distinct habitat preferences, the alder flycatchers nesting in alder swamps and streamside or lakeside thickets, while the willow flycatcher goes for swampy willow thickets and drier brushy clearings. Both feed primarily on flying insects in their respective habitats.

Eastern Wood-pewee

Contopus virens

Habitat: deciduous and mixed forest, forest edge
Food: terrestrial invertebrates, fruit
Nest Location: deciduous tree, 15–35′
Nest Type: cup
Length: 5.25″

More often heard whistling their name than seen in the dense forest canopy they frequent, eastern wood-pewees are yet another enigma for beginning bird watchers. Aside from their dull olive-gray backs and pair of pale wingbars on each wing, they simply have no other outstanding features. Were it not for their song, most of us would not even notice them as they forage, dashing from a favorite perch to snatch flying insects and returning to perch again.

Eastern and western wood-pewees are known among ornithologists as superspecies. Similar to the concept of sibling species discussed under willow flycatchers, superspecies are recent evolutionary entities that have descended from the same species, but in entirely separate geographical areas. To the observer, they can only be distinguished by song, a job made easier because their ranges do not overlap.

FAMILY ALAUDIDAE

Horned Lark

Eremophila alpestris

Habitat: field, prairie, beach, urban
Food: seeds, terrestrial invertebrates
Nest Location: ground
Nest Type: bowl
Length: 6.5″

These masked inhabitants of open areas are about as ubiquitous as land bird species get. Depending upon the season, they may be found from coast to coast and from arctic tundra to the Gulf of Mexico and the Rio Grande, and they are common throughout the rest of the northern hemisphere as well. They prefer spacious, barren ground, and are most often seen in places like beaches, freshly turned farm fields, grasslands, airports, and golf courses. In fall and winter, look for large flocks of tawny birds, each with a black brow, cheeks, and breast band superimposed over a yellow face and throat. They are often mixed with snow buntings, pipits, longspurs, and redpolls.

Members of this species flock together as a defense against predation, increasing the number of individuals watching and listening for danger and increasing the odds against any one individual being taken in an attack. Flocking also aids in foraging, overwhelming the territorial defenses of other species and increasing the chances that a rich feeding area will be located.

Horned larks are among our earliest nesters, and it is not uncommon for them to have established their nest of woven grasses at the base of a sedge or grass clump as early as February, with the intention of raising several broods that season. Like so many other birds of open terrain where trees are scarce, horned larks give their courtship song in flight. Circling at up to eight hundred feet, the male emits a sweet, tinkling melody, culminating with a closed-wing power dive back to the point of takeoff or nearby.

FAMILY HIRUNDINIDAE

Barn Swallow

Hirundo rustica

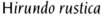

Habitat: farm, grassland, marsh, lake, suburban
Food: terrestrial invertebrates
Nest Location: building, bridge, cliff
Nest Type: cup
Length: 6″

For those lucky enough to have grown up in farm country, memories of summer certainly include hours watching the aerial acrobatics of barn swallows as they swoop, turn, and roll, covering up to an estimated 600 miles per day over nearby fields in pursuit of bountiful flying insects. Their grace and agility are gifts made possible by a long, forked tail. Such proficient aerialists are barn swallows that they even drink and bathe on the wing!

This is our only swallow with a deeply forked tail, quite evident in flight. They are colored steel-blue on their back and wings and a rusty cinnamon on their underparts, with a slightly darker throat. Colonial nesters, their constant twittering is a familiar sound around buildings within close proximity to fields, grassland, lakes, and marshes. Barn swallows prefer to nest in open buildings or under eaves, but may also build their mud nests under bridges or overhanging rock ledges near water, or in caves or culverts.

Tree Swallow

Tachycineta bicolor

Habitat: marsh, lake, river, field, forest edge
Food: terrestrial invertebrates
Nest Location: snag, nest, box, 3–10′
Nest Type: cavity
Length: 5″

The tree swallows' ability to feed on bayberries in the winter allows them to overwinter in large numbers as far north as coastal North Carolina and California. As a result, they are the first swallows to return to their summer range. In fall, just before migrating southward, tree swallows gather in great swarming flocks, putting on impressive aerial displays.

Tree swallows will nest in loose colonies if given the chance, but the availability of nest sites and competition from other cavity-nesters regulates this tendency. They prefer a cavity of nest box with the entrance facing open areas.

The foraging flights of tree swallows are characterized by circular glides, with each glide ending with several flaps and a short climb. Emerald flashes are emitted periodically as sunlight glances off the iridescent green backs of adults. This is our only swallow with a green back and solid white underparts. They have been observed chasing and playing with feathers and other wind-borne objects, an activity which may help hone their foraging skills.

Purple Martin

Progne subis

Habitat: field, grassland, desert, suburban
Food: terrestrial invertebrates
Nest Location: snag, 5–30′, nest box
Nest Type: cavity
Length: 7″

These strict cavity-nesters will make their home in abandoned woodpecker holes of natural chambers in a snag or cliff, but they are notorious for their preference of multi-unit apartment-style houses mounted on tall poles. Colonies of purple martins are in demand by many homeowners who erect martin houses in the hope of benefiting from the tremendous insect consumption of these flying vacuum cleaners. Even American Indians were known to covet their insect-eating ways, hanging hollow gourds for their homes from tall poles or saplings near their gardens.

Purple martins are more likely to take up residence if there is a body of water nearby where they can bathe and drink on the wing. These are our largest members of the swallow family. The all-dark males with their purple iridescence are unmistakable. Females, duller with gray breasts, may be confused with other swallows, but are larger and have broader wings.

Cliff Swallow

Hirundo pyrrhonota

Habitat: farm, river, lake, prairie, savanna
Food: terrestrial invertebrates
Nest Location: cliff, dam, bridge, building
Nest Type: ball
Length: 5″

The careful observer can learn to deduce the identity of swallows by their flight patterns. Cliff swallows, while foraging, tend to glide in long ellipses, with each glide ending in a steep climb. Up close, these square-tailed swallows are best told by their buffy rump patch, chestnut-brown throat, and white forehead.

These are the famed swallows which, according to folklore, are reputed to return to the Mission of El Capistrano, California, on the same day every year, resulting in joyful celebration by local residents. Colonies of their jug-shaped mud nests are commonly found plastered to the vertical surfaces of cliffs, dams, bridges, and buildings. The nests themselves, made from mud pellets, have a distinctly pebbled appearance. A short entrance tunnel leads to the spherical nest chamber.

Colonial nesting in such inaccessible locations provides refuge from most predators. The colony also serves as an informational clearing house for food sources. Unsuccessful foragers in the colony observe parents feeding nestlings and follow them on their next excursion. Cliff swallows may be observed feeding in mixed flocks.

FAMILY CORVIDAE

Blue Jay

Cyanocitta cristata

Habitat: deciduous, mixed, and coniferous forest, suburban
Food: fruit, nuts, seeds, terrestrial invertebrates, birds eggs, nestlings
Nest Location: conifer, 5–20′
Nest Type: cup
Length: 10″

Blue jays suffer an unsavory reputation as nest robbers that eat eggs and nestlings of woodland song birds. They may repay part of this debt, however, by acting as woodland sentries. Blue jays have a fierce dislike of predators, and when the stillness of the forest is shattered by their raucous alarm calls, it's likely that one such predator is afoot nearby. A skillful mimic, this rascal imitates the calls of hawks in order to drive small birds away from nests or feeders and into hiding. For the most part, they eat seeds, fruit, nuts, and insects. Like squirrels, blue jays tend to bury acorns in food caches and forget many of them, a trait which makes them part of the regeneration of oak forests.

Blue jays are beautifully marked, crested birds. Their bluish-gray face and underparts are interrupted by a black collar, while their back is patterned in white, black, and various shades of blue. It is an interesting side note that among the fabulous rainbow of colors in the bird world, there is no true blue pigment. While most colors of bird plumage are actually pigments infused at the molecular level, blues are the result of refracted light, light rays which are altered toward the blue end of the spectrum by the physical structure of feathers. You can demonstrate this with a molted blue jay feather. Immerse the blue feather in water, and it will appear gray as the denser medium changes the angle of the light rays.

Steller's Jay

Cyanocitta stelleri

Habitat: coniferous and mixed forest
Food: fruit, seeds, nuts, terrestrial invertebrates, bird eggs, nestlings
Nest Location: conifer, 8–25'
Nest Type: cup
Length: 11"

The Steller's jay is the western counterpart of the blue jay. The black plumage on the back and head of this crested bird blends into a beautiful azure on the rump and belly, while its wings and tail are adorned with shades of indigo and turquoise. Like its eastern cousin, the food preferences of the Steller's jay are eclectic, but it prefers acorns and pine seeds, which it stores in caches. It will raid the caches of acorn woodpeckers, which store their bounty in hole-riddled trees and fence posts.

Caching food and finding it again has been the subject of some study among ornithologists. Birds that breed where their preferred foods are only seasonally abundant must find ways of coping with the lean times. Some migrate to areas where food is plentiful throughout winter, but hazards of migration are many and the death toll high. Others change their diet to include whatever foods are available, but this is a gamble also. Still others hoard their favorite fare during times of plenty and retrieve it later. Finding those hidden stores of food again proves another challenge. It was once thought that birds fought their caches accidentally by random foraging in the same general areas, but studies have shown that the birds remember the location of their repositiories in relation to nearby landmarks. Moving the landmarks resulted in the birds' searches being displaced a corresponding distance.

Gray Jay

Perisoreus canadensis

Habitat: coniferous, mixed forest
Food: terrestrial invertebrates, fruit, carrion, bird eggs
Nest Location: conifer, 4–30'
Nest Type: cup
Length: 10"

Better known as camp robber or whiskey-jack (from the Algonquin Indian name "wiskedjak"), a gray jay is the supreme opportunist. Though its diet consists chiefly of insects, fruit, and carrion, it is notorious for its brazen acts in stealing food from hunters and campers. Reports of this bird landing on plates or even frying pans during meals and snatching bits of food are not uncommon. The report of a rifle or shotgun is also known to lure them, eager for scraps of fresh meat.

Gray jay's insatiable appetites stem from their need to build up large fat reserves and food caches to help them survive the severe northern and western winters and to begin nesting as early as late February. It is their way of coping with the uneven food supplies of their year-round range.

Aptly named, the plumage of this species is a study in grays. Its back, wings and tail are medium gray, the breast is light gray, and its throat and forehead are whitish. The gray jay's most prominent field mark is the black patch on the nape of its neck.

Black-billed Magpie

Pica pica

Habitat: prairie, coniferous and riparian forest, thicket, farm
Food: terrestrial invertebrates, carrion, fruit, seeds, bird eggs, nestlings, small mammals
Nest Location: deciduous tree, shrub, 20–30'
Nest Type: ball
Length: 18"

Its colors are reminiscent of a circus clown, and the black-billed magpie is just as full of mischief. Rare is the western resident or visitor who is not familiar with the antics of these long-tailed corvids. Like other members of their family, magpies demonstrate a considerable degree of intelligence and resourcefulness, and they are not above using all of their wits to panhandle food around houses or campgrounds, or to steal it if the handouts are not forthcoming. They've also shown an affinity for shiny metallic objects like jewel-

ry. Some consider them vermin for their habits of raiding bird nests and grain fields, but in reality their effect on a grain harvest is minimal and most of the species whose nests they raid are resilient enough to re-nest successfully. A large portion of their diet consists of insects, rodents, and carrion, so they are beneficial to us.

Magpies are large birds with bold black-and-white markings, white wing patches, and a ridiculously long, streaming tail. Its multi-colored wings and tail in sunlight will rival a rainbow. Its nest, a cup of mud lined with hair, grass, and rootlets, is surrounded by a veritable fortress constructed of sticks and secured by a roof of thorny twigs.

Common Raven

Corvus corax

Habitat: coniferous forest, alpine tundra, desert
Food: carrion, small mammals, bird eggs, nestlings, reptiles, fruit, terrestrial invertebrates
Nest Location: cliff, conifer, 20–100'
Nest Type: cup
Length: 21"

The corvid family, which includes crows, ravens, jays, and magpies, show the greatest brain development of any birds, and among these, the raven is arguably the most intelligent of all. These ebony spirits are given to performing spectacular swoops, barrel rolls, and other aerial acrobatics for no apparent reason, contributing to their reputation for playfulness. They also have a

long history in the legends and folklore of peoples in the northern hemisphere, including, not surprisingly, links to magical phenomena. The first scientific reference to ravens was probably that made by the great Greek philosopher and scientist, Aristotle, about 350BC, when he described their feeding territories.

Coal black with a pleasing sheen, ravens differ from crows by their baritone calls, heavier bills, larger size, and thick, shaggy throat. In flight, their unmistakably wedge-shaped tails are diagnostic. These ominivorous scavengers nest in remote locations, such as cliffs or trees, and do not tolerate civilization.

American Crow

Corvus brachyrhynchos

Habitat: deciduous, mixed, coniferous, and riparian forest, field, prairie, suburban
Food: terrestrial invertebrates, carrion, reptiles, amphibians, bird eggs, nestlings, seeds, fruit, nuts
Nest Location: deciduous tree, shrub, 1–70′
Nest Type: cup
Length: 17″

Wary, intelligent, adaptable, omnivorous, and prolific, the American crow is armed with every trait needed to flourish in man-altered environments. When a group of crows is feeding, there is always at least one sentinel in nearby trees watching for any hint of danger. Crows become quite

incensed by the presence of birds of prey, particularly great horned owls that regularly attack crow roosts. Upon spotting a great horned owl, a flock of crows becomes a rag-ing mob in relentless pursuit of their enemy until it either escapes or takes cover in dense tree tops.

When not nesting, these coal-black birds regularly congregate in communal roosts. This is a clear case of you-scratch-my-back-and-I'll-scratch-yours. Young and inexperienced crows roost with their elders in order to follow them to the best foraging areas by day. The more experienced birds tolerate this because, being more dominant, they are able to commandeer the more protected and more central positions within the roost. The older crows' increased safety from nocturnal great horned owl attacks, outweighs the greater competition for food with younger birds by day. Similarly, the younger crows as a group gain more from the better foraging than they lose from assuming the riskier positions on the perimeter of the roost.

FAMILY PARIDAE

Black-capped Chickadee

Parus atricapillus

Habitat: deciduous, mixed, and riparian forest, thickets, suburban
Food: terrestrial invertebrates, seeds, fruits
Nest Location: deciduous tree, snag, nest box, 4–10′
Nest Type: cavity
Length: 4.5″

Nothing lifts one's spirits on a frigid winter day so much as the sight of these uninhibited bundles of energy nimbly flitting about feeders and leafless trees as if they hadn't even noticed the cold. Even though they appear to be the embodiment of cheerfulness in the bleakest of seasons, these black-headed little birds with their white cheeks and tawny flanks are actually engaged in the serious game of survival, and through the winter they are often poised on the brink of starvation.

In late summer after the chicks have fledged, mated pairs of chickadees begin to band together, forming roving groups of usually 8–12 birds that establish and patrol a feeding territory. It is their method of coping with the rigors of winter, for it multiplies, by whatever the number of birds in the flock, the number of eyes searching for food sources and watching for possible danger. As the group fans out on feeding forays through the forest, each member gives periodic high-pitched calls that keep the flock together even when they are out of one another's sight. The familiar "chickadeedee" call for which they are named is a rallying cry that brings the flock back together after they have been dispersed by some disturbance.

Within each flock there are usually several "floaters", unmated birds that change flocks often. A chickadee's life span is fairly short, and when one member of a pair dies, a floater or another bird that has also lost its mate will step in to fill the void. In a social hierarchy such as the chickadee's where the more dominant individuals are more successful in reproducing, this is a way of quickly enhancing one's position within the system, or, at the very least, of obtaining a new mate to retain one's present position.

Tufted Titmouse

Parus bicolor

Habitat: deciduous,
mixed, and riparian forest,
thicket, suburban
Food: terrestrial
invertebrates, seeds, nuts,
fruit
Nest Location:
deciduous tree, snag,
3–90', nest box
Nest Type: cavity
Length: 5.5"

This bright-eyed woodland sprite is a very attractive bird with its perpetually erect crest, gray back, and peach-colored flanks. The beady eyes set in a whitish face convey an air of alertness, a definite trait of the tufted titmouse.

Just as black-capped chickadees band together to enhance their abilities to forage and spot danger, tufted titmouse benefit similarly from joining a group. Their numbers are fewer than chickadees, so rather than forming their own band, they enlist in a flock of chickadees, their near relatives. In fact, if you sight tufted titmice in winter, its a sure bet that a gang of black-capped chickadees is nearby. These two species often constitute part of a larger mixed flock that also includes woodpeckers, nuthatches, brown creepers, and kinglets, all cooperating in foraging and defense for the sake of individual survival.

Tufted titmice are warier than chickadees; they are usually the first to detect predators and their shrill alarm alerts their compatriots, who immediately freeze and begin to utter thin, ventriloquistic notes that mask their locations. Chickadees tolerate titmice for the added security of a vigilant sentry while the titmouse has an easier time filling its belly with the aid of the chickadees.

FAMILY SITTIDAE

White-breasted Nuthatch

Sitta carolinensis

Habitat: deciduous,
mixed, and riparian forest,
forest edge, suburban
Food: terrestrial
invertebrates, seeds, nuts
Nest Location:
deciduous tree, snag,
10–60', nest box
Nest Type: cavity
Length: 5"

With their boldly marked faces and comical antics, it's easy to characterize nuthatches as the clowns of woodland birds. Their name is derived from an old European name, "nut-hack", from their habit of wedging seeds and nuts in a crevice and hammering away with a chisel-like bill until they open.

They are also the only birds that habitually move head first down the trunk of a tree. Since woodpeckers scour the same tree trunks from the base upward, they overlook food hidden in upward-facing bark fissures. As they descend the trunk, nuthatches spot these missed titbits and thus are able to coexist with woodpeckers while exploiting the same resources. Together with other bark-gleaners like chickadees, titmice, kinglets, and brown creepers, nuthatches and woodpeckers form an association known to ecologists as a guild, a group of species in the same habitat that utilize the same resources in similar but not identical manners.

White-breasted nuthatches are common feeder visitors, where their favorite fare is sunflower seeds. In the wild they subsist on

insects, acorns, hickory nuts, beech nuts, and assorted other seeds. The jet-black cap of the male is the only field mark that distinguishes it from the gray-capped female, who has the same white face and breast and slate-gray back.

Red-breasted Nuthatch

Sitta canadensis

Habitat: coniferous and mixed forest
Food: terrestrial invertebrates, seeds, fruit
Nest Location: conifer, snag, 6–60', nest box
Nest Type: cavity
Length: 4"

Though similar in behavior to their white-breasted cousins of deciduous woodlands, red-breasted nuthatches show a strong preference for conifers. The male's black eye line and black cap are separated by a white eye stripe. He's also got a white throat, gray back, and a rusty belly and breast. Females are paler, more muted versions of the males.

It is their affinity for pine seeds that make coniferous and mixed forests the haunt of red-breasted nuthatches. In addition to insects and their eggs, these sprites will also consume berries. Periodic food shortages over large geographical areas cause irruptions of red-breasted nuthatches and several other northern seed-eating species, in which birds that would normally winter on their breeding grounds instead make southward invasions in the autumn. Often a failure of the coniferous cone crop is preceded by a year of abundance, therefore resulting in a population increase of coniferous seed-eaters and additional pressure to migrate *en masse* when faced with a food shortage.

Red-breasted nuthatches are easily lured to feeders, where they take the universally-popular offering, sunflower seeds. Both they and white-breasted nuthatches may seem anti-social, preferring to quickly snatch a seed and dash off to some nearby tree, but don't be offended. The adductor muscles that close their bills are not strong enough to simply crush the hull of the seed, and their feet, adapted to cling to vertical surfaces, are not dexterous enough to hold the seed on a perch while they open it. They simply seek a crack in which to wedge

the seed so they can chisel away at the hull with the tip of their bill until the tasty interior is exposed.

FAMILY TROGLODYTIDAE

House Wren

Troglodytes aedon

Habitat: forest edge, thicket, suburban, farm
Food: terrestrial invertebrates
Nest Location: deciduous tree, snag, 1–20', nest box
Nest Type: cavity
Length: 4.25"

What the house wren lacks in decorative plumage, it more than makes up for with its bubbly, exuberant song reminiscent of a gurgling country brook. The common trait of wrens is their habit of holding their tail cocked perpetually skyward. The house wren is distinguished from most other wrens by its lack of field marks.

House wrens are normally found close to human habitation, where they perform a valuable service by gleaning large numbers of insects, many of them pests, from the foliage of plants. Though they are bold enough to appropriate nest cavities from other small birds, they are remarkably flexible in their domestic requirements. Reports of house wrens nesting in such unlikely places as pockets of clothing hung out to dry, rain spouts, mailboxes, flower pots, drain pipes, tin cans, and even a cow skull are not uncommon. They also take easily to nest boxes. Most nest boxes need to be cleaned out before the nesting season begins, but house wrens are not above doing their own spring housecleaning. They will dismantle an old nest twig by twig and proceed to build a new one, often using many pieces from the original nest.

FAMILY MIMIDAE

Northern Mockingbird

Mimus polyglottos

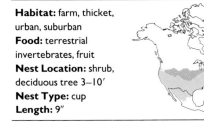

Habitat: farm, thicket, urban, suburban
Food: terrestrial invertebrates, fruit
Nest Location: shrub, deciduous tree 3–10′
Nest Type: cup
Length: 9″

If there is a bird more accurately named than the mockingbird, I don't know of it. The northern mockingbird is gifted with a truly remarkable vocal range. It seems able to effectively mimic nearly every bird song or call it hears, often randomly piecing together a long string of sounds roughly equivalent to a human mixing words from about 20 different languages to recite a single verse of a poem. It is no wonder that the northern mockingbird was assigned a scientific name which, translated, means "mimic of many tongues".

Otherwise gray mockingbirds have bold, white "flash patterns" on their wings and outer tail feathers that are mostly hidden at rest but flash conspicuously when the bird takes flight. The major purpose of these field marks is to distract predators, especially snakes, from the vicinity of the nest. Mockingbirds are also reputed to use these flash patterns to startle insects, one of their primary foods, into flight from their hiding places in the grass.

Gray Catbird

Dumetella carolinensis

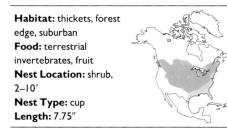

Habitat: thickets, forest edge, suburban
Food: terrestrial invertebrates, fruit
Nest Location: shrub, 2–10′
Nest Type: cup
Length: 7.75″

Gray catbirds, though closely related to mockingbirds, have not quite mastered the art of vocal impressions to the same degree as they have. Instead, they sound a lot more like the droid R2-D2 of "Star Wars" movie fame. They are named for their mewing call, one sound they can mimic rather convincingly.

Catbirds skulk about in dense brush, rarely providing an unobstructed view of themselves. They are plain, slate-gray birds except for a black cap and a patch of burnt umber under the base of a long tail.

In a parenting strategy that we may consider cold, but that works well for the catbirds, a female will begin incubating before completing her clutch so that the eggs hatch at different times. The older chicks are larger and stronger than their younger siblings, and better able to get the lion's share of the insects delivered by their parents. This ensures that as many offspring survive as the food supply will support. During times of plenty, all of the chicks should receive enough to eat, but were they all to hatch at the same time during a lean season, distributing the limited food supply evenly could threaten the entire brood.

Wood Thrush

Hylocichla mustelina

Habitat: deciduous woodland, mixed woodland
Food: terrestrial invertebrates, fruit
Nest Location: deciduous tree, conifer, 6–50′
Nest Type: cup
Length: 7″

Perhaps the sweetest song of North American birds is the flutelike melody of a woodthrush as it drifts through mature eastern deciduous woodlands at dawn, an ageless song reminding us of a time when virgin forests covered much of the same area. Slightly smaller than a robin, wood thrushes have a rusty head and upper back, fading into medium brown wings and tail, and a heavily spotted white breast. They feed heavily on insects and berries in the shade of the forest floor, but will also take earthworms and spiders.

Wood thrushes are close relatives of robins, and as such they build similar cup-shaped nests of mud, grass, leaves, and barks, but with one notable diference. Wherever possible, they will incorporate scraps of white paper, cloth, plastic, or natural materials. Some naturalists believe this practice helps the incubating female's white spotted breast blend with the nest, thus breaking up her outline and rendering her loss conspicuous in the sun-dappled forest understory.

Brown Thrasher

Toxostoma rufum

Habitat: thickets, suburban, forest edge
Food: terrestrial invertebrates, amphibians, reptiles, fruit, nuts
Nest Location: shrub, ground, 0–5′
Nest Type: cup
Length: 10″

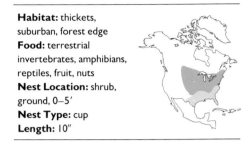

Mockingbirds are conspicuous in song, singing oft-repeated phrases from an exposed perch. Catbirds are less bold, repeating each phrase only once from the cover of shrubbery, but giving themselves away when they mew. Brown thrashers, on the other hand, can be downright uncooperative. They are secretive mimics except at the peak of the breeding season, but they sing in couplets, twice-repeated phrases that give them away.

Despite their apparent modesty and limited mimicry skills, it has been found that male brown thrashers have the largest known long repertoire of all North American bird species, an arsenal of more than 1,100 documented melodies, and estimated at more than 3,000. This is quite an accomplishment, considering that, unlike calls, which are instinctive, songs must be learned from others. The vocal versatility of a male apparently plays a large part in determining his place in the brown thrasher hierarchy, the quality of territory he is able to claim and his success in luring a mate.

It has been said that, "a brown thrasher looks like a wood thrush that has been stretched". If you've ever seen a wood thrash, you'd consider this a pretty fair description. Brown thrashers are long and slim, rufous above with a white, heavily streaked breast and a long tail. They forage for food on the ground, sweeping their heavy bills from side to side to expose the bare soil underneath dead leaves.

Hermit Thrush

Catharus guttatus

Habitat: coniferous and mixed forest, forest edge, swamp
Food: terrestrial invertebrates, amphibians, fruit
Nest Location: ground, deciduous tree, conifer, 0–8′
Nest Type: cup
Length: 6″

A shy, retiring bird is the hermit thrush, just like its namesake. Moist coniferous forests are the favored home of the "swamp angel", as it has been called. Its liquid, melodius improvisations are thought by some to rival or exceed those of the wood thrush in pure beauty. When this ground dweller does show itself amid the lush vegetation of its home, one finds it hard to believe that such beautiful music originates from such a plain bird. Its olive-brown back blends gradually into a russet tail, the reverse of a wood thrush's coloration, and the spots concentrated on the upper breast are more diffuse than those of a wood thrush. The best field mark is the bird's habit of cocking its tail above its back, slowly lowering it, and flicking it erect once again.

Hermit thrushes are among a number of songbird species that have been observed engaged in a process known as anting. The birds pick up single ants or several at a time and rub them on their feathers. Some even spread their wings and squirm atop an ant hill to encourage ants to climb up into their plumage. The reason for this behavior is not fully understood among ornithologists, but it is theorized that the birds who do this benefit from the secretions of ants, which are known to have bactericidal, fungicidal, and insecticidal properties. Mites are a serious problem to birds, and these too are repelled by ant secretions.

American Robin

Turdus migratorius

Habitat: urban, suburban, farm, deciduous and mixed forest
Food: terrestrial invertebrates, fruits
Nest Location: deciduous tree, conifer, 10'–20', buildings
Nest Type: cup
Length: 8.5"

Arguably the best known bird in North America, American robins are recognized as *the* sign of spring when they return north from their wintering grounds. For at least part of the year, they are common on lawns from Alaska to Florida. With its brick-red breast, sooty back, and black head, a male robin is easy to identify even if one does not notice its white eye ring or the small white triangles on each corner of its tail. Females are paler versions of males.

Though their diet includes a wide range of invertebrates and fruit, earthworms are the best known element in their diet. It's been reported that robins eat up to 14 feet of earthworms per day, but how researchers measure these elastic critters or why they would bother is a mystery.

Anyone who has spent time watching robins hunt has noticed them cocking their heads from one side to another as if listening for the telltale rustlings of their prey. In actuality, robins hunt purely by sight. Birds' eyes are fixed in their sockets, so in order to focus on different objects, the bird must turn its head. Robins have basically monocular vision, which means that each eye can function independently of the other, and with their eyes placed high on the sides of their heads they are well equipped to detect the approach of predators. In order to scan the ground for prey, however, a robin must cock its head at an extreme angle, giving the impression that it is listening, not looking.

Eastern Bluebird

Sialia sialis

Habitat: farm, prairie, orchard, forest edge
Food: terrestrial invertebrates, fruit
Nest Location: snag, 2–50', nest box
Nest Type: cavity
Length: 5.5"

For the male's breath-taking turquoise hue and the species' underdog status against such unsavory aggressors as European starlings, the eastern bluebird could well be America's favorite bird. These country residents are voracious insect eaters who benefit farmers and homeowners alike, as well as gracing all observers with their beauty. Though duller on the back, head, and wings, the female shares the male's rusty breast and sides.

With the possible exception of wood ducks, no other North American species has benefited so much from ambitious recovery programs. With their population in serious decline due to pesticide poisoning, food shortages, and stiff competition for fewer and fewer nest sites, eastern bluebirds have fended off possible extinction, thanks to reduced pesticide usage and massive numbers of nest boxes erected in suitable locations by farmers, birdwatchers, and homeowners. Although they are now on the rebound, even common in some areas where they sit hunched on fences and telephone wires, this species can still benefit from more nest boxes placed around the perimeter of fields, meadows, and pastures. Nest boxes should have entrance holes of exactly one and one-half inches to exclude starlings and should be at least 8 inches deep to foil cats. Guidelines for nest boxes are mentioned in Chapter 2.

Mountain Bluebird

Sialia currocoides

Habitat: coniferous and deciduous forest, subalpine meadow
Food: terrestrial invertebrates, fruit
Nest Location: snag, 2–50', nest box
Nest Type: cavity
Length: 6"

Mountain bluebird males match the brilliant blue of western skies with their plumage. Females, while duller on the head and back, share this cerulean hue on their rump, tail, and tinged on their wings. During the breeding season, mountain bluebirds are most vocal with their warbling song before sunrise, for which reason the Navajo people called them "heralds of the rising sun".

During the summer mountain bluebirds are found from mountain foothills, where sagebrush and forests meet, to subalpine meadows, where they can be seen hovering about shrubs while gleaning insects from their limbs and foliage. They descend from higher elevations to winter in the southern grasslands and deserts of North America. Like the eastern bluebird, this species has also declined in numbers, due primarily to competition for nest sites from house sparrows and European starlings.

Mountain bluebirds lend themselves well to a discussion of color. Most colors found among birds are the result of pigments, molecular compounds that absorb certain wavelengths of light and reflect others. Blues and iridescent colors among birds, however, are not produced by pigments. Rather, they are produced by minute structures on the feather that are smaller than the wavelength of red light. These scatter shorter wavelengths in all directions, causing them to appear blue when viewed at any angle in reflected light. Iridescent colors are produced by feathers with modified barbules on the feathers that reflect some wavelengths and absorb others. The reflected light changes in wavelength with the viewing angle, hence the rainbow effect that seems to move across a bird's plumage.

FAMILY CERTHIIDAE

Brown Creeper

Certhia americana

Habitat: coniferous, mixed, deciduous forest, suburban
Food: terrestrial invertebrates, nuts, seeds
Nest Location: conifer, deciduous tree, 3–50'
Nest Type: cup
Length: 4.75"

The brown creeper keeps a low profile and is therefore often not recognized as a common woodland species. Its mottled brown back and head blend perfectly with its usual bark backdrop, and the thin, high-pitched calls it emits are barely audible to humans even at close range. The most identifying trait of this unobtrusive bird is the spiral path it takes around a tree trunk as it climbs up woodpecker-style, with stiff tail feathers braced against the trunk for support. Its thin, slightly down-curved bill is undoubtedly an aid in gleaning insects from odd-shaped crevices that the heavier, straight bills of woodpeckers and nuthatches do not reach.

One of the more interesting aspects of brown creeper life is its nest-building. The nest, a cup of woven moss, twigs, and bark strips slung like a hammock behind a loose flap of bark. For the most part, the tree must be dead or dying for the bark to peel away in such a fashion, but the shagbark hickory, with its naturally curling bark slabs, is in great demand among brown creepers where their two ranges overlap.

This type of nest is more vulnerable than either a cavity or a nest hidden by foliage, so the bird must be inconspicuous as it approaches in order to avoid drawing attention to it. Enter the camouflage plumage and quiet nature of our hero, the brown creeper. As the bird inches toward the nest, spiraling from around the trunk and slipping under the bark, it seems simply to vanish. Upon emerging, it takes a spiral route away from the nest to lessen the likelihood of being spotted near the entrance.

FAMILY SYLVIIDAE

Ruby-crowned Kinglet

Regulus calendula

Habitat: coniferous, mixed, and deciduous forest, thicket
Food: terrestrial invertebrates, tree sap, fruit, seeds
Nest Location: conifer, 15–30'
Nest Type: basket
Length: 3.5"

The scarlet crown for which this species is named is rarely visible and is flashed by the male only during courtship or aggressive displays. Aside from the ruby patch on the head of the male, these olive-gray midgets show few other field marks except for a white eye ring and white wing bars. Adding to a bird watcher's frustration with ruby-crowned kinglets is their penchant for remaining high in dense conifers. The nervous flick of their wings as they hope from one limb to another and their thin, scratchy

call are often the only clues which indicate their presence.

A ruby-crowned kinglet's diet consists chiefly of insects and spiders, but they take more seeds and berries in the winter. They also supplement their diet with tree sap that leaks from woodpecker workings or from naturally occurring injuries to trees.

Their nests are tightly woven baskets of lichens, mosses, and plant fibers bound with spider silk and suspended from a limb. For aid in foraging and protection against predators, they often join mixed-species flocks in the fall which may include golden-crowned kinglets, brown creepers, titmice, chickadees, and nuthatches.

FAMILY BOMBYCILLIDAE

Cedar Waxwing

Bombycilla cedrorum

Habitat: deciduous and mixed forest, forest edge, orchard, suburban
Food: fruit, terrestrial invertebrates, tree sap
Nest Location: deciduous tree, conifer, 6–50'
Nest Type: cup
Length: 5.75"

Field marks abound on a cedar waxwing, from its black Lone Ranger-style mask on a crested head to its golden-brown body and terminal lemon-yellow tail band. Less visible are the waxy red spots on its wings for

which it is named. The function of these droplets, discharges from the shafts of specialized secondary flight feathers, is undetermined, but they may indicate age and help establish social status.

Except when nesting, cedar waxwings roam the countryside in flocks, marking their location with a frequent high-pitched, ringing trill. They are gluttonous fruit eaters that, in a flock, can make short work of stripping a fruit tree. They have been observed lined up on a branch or fence, passing berries down the line from one to another. They sometimes partake of fermented fruit and eat themselves into a drunken stupor. As fond as they are of fruit, cedar waxwings instinctively feed their newly hatched offspring large quantities of protein-rich insects for the first few days in order to nourish their rapid growth during this period.

FAMILY STURNIDAE

European Starling

Sturnus vulgaris

Habitat: urban, suburban, farm, forest edge
Food: terrestrial invertebrates, fruit, seeds
Nest Location: deciduous tree, snag, 10–25', building, nest box
Nest Type: cavity
Length: 6"

The European starling represents a classic case of what may happen when one thoughtlessly tampers with nature. In 1890, a zealous fan of Shakespeare embarked upon a moronic mission to introduce into North America all of the birds mentioned in Shakespearean works, perhaps in the belief that they would inspire our cultural development. That year, he imported 60 starlings from England and released them in New York City's Central Park, followed by another 40 starlings the following year. The 200,000,000+ starlings plaguing our native cavity-nesting birds coast to coast today, having caused dramatic declines in the populations of many, have all descended from those original 100 birds.

Adding insult to injury, European starlings have few redeeming qualities to offer in compensation for the species they've displaced. These stocky black birds have a perpetually greasy appearance and a raucous, irritating call. Large flocks devastate grain fields in the country and foul cars, sidewalks, and buildings in the city. That they also consume many insects is a minor reward for our tolerance of them.

Stubby-tailed starlings are easily identified by their waddling stride and clamorous din. Their bill, yellow in summer, turns black in winter as their black plumage becomes speckled with white spots.

FAMILY VIREONIDAE

Red-eyed Vireo

Vireo olivaceus

Habitat: deciduous forest, suburbs
Food: terrestrial invertebrates, fruit
Nest Location: shrub, deciduous tree, 5–35'
Nest Type: basket
Length: 5"

This songster was once considered one of the most common birds of eastern deciduous woodlands, but its numbers are declining and its status uncertain due to the fragmentation of North American forests where it nests, the destruction of the Amazonian rainforest where it spends the winter, pesticide poisoning, and nest parasitism by brown-headed cowbirds.

Cowbird nest parasitism is a serious problem for many woodland songbirds, but particularly for the red-eyed vireo, who seems unable to distinguish a cowbird egg from its own. Not only that, but the problem is worsening. Cowbirds are primarily residents of the forest edge. With housing developments and logging carving up North American forests and increasingly exposing the forest interior, cowbirds are finding more hosts, while their victims have fewer places to escape them. A cowbird egg placed clandestinely in the nest while the parents are absent will, if not discarded, hatch before the legitimate offspring, giving the greedy cowbird chick a headstart on its foster siblings. The late-comers are outmuscled for the food their parents deliver and seldom survive. This is a serious setback for birds that winter in the tropics, because they have only one shot at nesting success each year before they must again depart southward.

Red-eyed vireos are tireless singers during their nesting season, starting in the pre-dawn hours and continuing almost non-stop through dusk. One, under surveillance by a researcher, reportedly sang 22,197 songs in one day. The fact that their songs consist of only two syllables undoubtedly contributed to this record.

This is a bird of the forest canopy, and diligent effort is required to catch a clear view of it. Its eyes are red, of course, but the gray cap, white eye stripe bordered with black, and olive-gray back make much better field marks. It is easier identified by song than by sight.

FAMILY PARULIDAE

Yellow Warbler

Dendroica petechia

Habitat: thicket, swamp, stream, suburban, orchard
Food: terrestrial invertebrates
Nest Location: shrub, deciduous tree, 1–14'
Nest Type: cup
Length: 4"

The waves of migrating warblers that sweep northward across North America every spring are a genuine treat for bird watchers. At some vantage points it is not unusual to spot more than a dozen species of these colorful little birds in a few hours of looking, a fine reward for the limited birding opportunities of a long winter.

Yellow warblers are common and can hardly be missed if you look for them in moist thickets and along brushy streams. They are canary-yellow in color, and in fact they resemble miniature canaries except for the chestnut streaks on the male's breast and sides. During the breeding season, males will proclaim sovereignty over their territory from the tops of snags or trees with thin foliage.

Yellow warbler nests are also frequent cowbird targets, but fortunately yellow warblers are more discriminating about their eggs than some other migrants, and they usually respond by building another layer over the old eggs and re-nesting. They seem willing to do this as often as is necessary until they end up with a clutch that is cowbird-free.

Yellow-rumped Warbler

Dendroica coronata

Habitat: coniferous and mixed forest
Food: terrestrial invertebrates, fruit
Nest Location: conifer, 4–50'
Nest Type: ??
Length: 4.25"

The field marks of a yellow-rumped warbler are easy to recognize. The back of a male is gun-metal blue and streaked with black. He has a white throat, a black breast band, and distinct yellow patches on the shoulders, crown, and rump (the throat of the western race is yellow, also). Females are similarly marked, but with a brownish back instead of the blue of the mate.

The eastern race of this species was formerly known as the myrtle warbler, named for its fondness for the berries of wax myrtle and bayberry bushes. These berries have a waxy coating that most animals cannot digest, but the digestive systems of yellow-rumped warblers are equipped with enzymes specially for this purpose. This ability allows yellow-rumped warblers to winter as far north as coastal areas of Washington and Massachusetts, and consequently they are the first warblers to arrive on their summer range.

Chestnut-sided Warbler

Dendroica pensylvanica

Habitat: thickets, forest edge
Food: terrestrial invertebrates, fruit
Nest Location: shrub, 1–3'
Nest Type: cup
Length: 4.25"

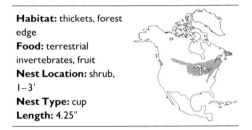

The carving up of large tracts of north American forests by loggers and developers is viewed with much consternation by environmentalists, but one species that's not complaining is the chestnut-sided warbler. These are inhabitants of the forest edge, and every small clearing cut in the woods means more habitat available to them. They also benefited from the abandoned, brushy fields and pastures of farms that failed during hard times. Like yellow warblers, chestnut-sided warblers are frequent cowbird hosts, and they deal with the problem in similar fashion.

Chestnut-sided warblers are just that, with a streak of rich chestnut running the length of each side from throat to flank, somewhat less distinct on females than on males. A white breast, white cheeks, a lemon-yellow crown, and a black boomerang through each eye complete their notable field marks. Their chief food is insects that they glean from foliage and twigs or catch on the wing.

Common Yellowthroat

Geothlypis trichas

Habitat: thicket, forest edge, farm, marsh, salt marsh, swamp
Food: terrestrial invertebrates
Nest Location: shrub, 0–3'
Nest Type: cup
Length: 4.25"

Their summer range stretches from coast to coast and from the Northwest Territories to the Gulf of Mexico, making the common yellowthroat one of our most widespread warblers. It is certainly one of the most abundant, also, especially in the wet brushy habitats they prefer. Look for them in thickets bordering streams, lakes, marshes, and swamps. In the tangled brush they may be difficult to see, but they are quite possessive about their territory and will emerge to scold any intruder. A soft squeaking sound made by kissing the back of one's hand will agitate the bird even further, usually drawing it out into full view, where the lemon-yellow breast and black bandit-like mask make you wonder how you'd missed it before.

Like people, birds such as the common yellowthroat with a wide geographic distribution often exhibit regional variations in their dialect; an accent, if you will. While the basic quality of the song leaves the bird's identity indisputable, assorted inflections or extra syllables may be thrown in anywhere, resulting in some interesting variations.

During the breeding season, these little birds are pumped so full of hormones that they sometimes cannot contain themselves and burst into song in the middle of the night. At other times they may rise on fluttering wings, bubbling over with unpredictable songs quite different from their usual melodies. These are called ecstasy songs and seem to function mainly as an emotional release or to vent nervous energy.

American Redstart

Setophaga ruticilla

Habitat: deciduous and mixed forest, forest edge
Food: terrestrial invertebrates
Nest Location: deciduous tree, shrub, 10–20'
Nest Type: cup
Length: 4.5"

American redstarts are often described as "nervous" due to the constant flicking of their wings and tail as they hop almost nonstop through the branches of a tree. All this motion is really just a foraging technique, quite effective for the redstart. As the male flicks his wings and tail, he is actually flashing his famous orange wing and tail patches, which seem all the brighter against the contrasting black of his upper plumage (females have similar but paler markings). These actions seem to startle insects into taking flight from their hiding places, and the redstart is then able to snatch them from mid-air flycatcher-style. They've even got bristles around the mouth, modified feathers that enhance their sensation of touch, just like those of flycatchers. Such bristles aid them in capturing flying insects.

In between airborne treats such as these, they glean the more sedentary insects from foliage and twigs.

Birds like the American redstart are good examples of the link between ecological succession and wildlife. Ecological succession is the process by which plants colonize a disturbed area and change its characteristics, making it more hospitable for other plants than for themselves. In this fashion, plant communities change gradually until a stable system, known as a climax community, is attained. Wildlife populations also change; species appear and disappear with the plant communities upon which they depend. American redstarts are inhabitants of young woodlands. Left alone, a cleared forest will revert from grassland to a shrub community to saplings, and as the saplings grow taller, American redstarts move in and stay until the forest approaches its climax stage, at which time they are gradually replaced by a species favoring the more mature community.

FAMILY ICTERIDAE

Bobolink

Dolichonyx oryzivorus

Habitat: field, grassland
Food: terrestrial invertebrates, seeds
Nest Location: ground
Nest Type: cup
Length: 6"

A strict denizen of grasslands and fields, the bobolink was undoubtedly a summer resident only in the prairies of central North America until the European settlers began clearing forested areas for agriculture. At one time, during their fall migration back to their winter range in Argentina and Brazil, they would descend in massive flocks onto South Carolina rice plantations to refuel. Irate rice farmers slaughtered untold numbers of them, never realizing that these "rice birds" were really bobolinks in drab winter plumage, the same birds that, in small mixed flocks of boldly-marked males and mottled females, feasted on dandelion seeds during their spring passage. This carnage, combined with disappearing farmland and the earlier harvesting of hayfields, caused a reduction in their population from which they have not recovered.

Dense grasses and herbs are required cover for the nests of bobolinks. While strolling through such areas, you may flush a female and think it easy to find her nest, but she disguises her retreat by running a distance from the nest before taking flight. Males are the only North American land bird whose plumage is dark below and light above. Up close, one can see their black breast and face and their golden nape. The white shoulder patches and rump are visible at rest and in flight.

Yellow-headed Blackbird

Xanthocephalus xanthocephalus

Habitat: freshwater marsh
Food: terrestrial invertebrates, seeds
Nest Location: reeds, 0.5–3′
Nest Type: cup
Length: 8.5″

Every spring, western marshes resound with the din of huge flocks of blackbirds, both yellow-headed and red-winged. The two species are self-descriptive and easy to tell apart, but the fact that they coexist in the same habitats at the same time and eating the same foods makes for an interesting investigation.

When two or more species compete for exactly the same resources, one of three things will happen. In an even match, both species may evolve so as to become less dependent upon the mutual requirement. Or, one species may dominate while the other evolves to take advantage of alternative resources or moves to a different region. In the last scenario, one species emerges as dominant while the other, unable to adapt, is driven to extinction.

Yellow-headed and red-winged blackbirds have apparently come to agree on the second option. In spring, red-winged males arrive earlier and occupy entire marshes. When the larger yellow-headed males arrive later, they usurp the best territories, those areas over deeper water that support cattails and nurture more insect life. Red-winged blackbirds have adapted to nest successfully in the less-productive territories around the marsh perimeter where their yellow-headed cousins cannot cope. The larger size of yellow-headed blackbirds, which allows them to evict red-wings, may be the result of natural selection, their larger ancestors having bred most successfully.

Common Grackle

Quiscalus quiscula

Habitat: farm, suburban
Food: terrestrial invertebrates, fruit, seeds, nuts, amphibians, bird eggs, nestlings
Nest Location: conifer, 2–20′
Nest Type: cup
Length: 11″

Common grackles may seem like just another black bird, but appearances can be deceiving. Under the right conditions, especially in direct sunlight, the glossy plumage of males shimmers with muted iridescence, especially purples, blues, greens, and bronze. The feathers of females are less glossy. The oddly keeled tails of common grackles also distinguish them from most other black birds.

One's attention is drawn to their bright yellow eyes. The irises of many birds' eyes are dark. What, then, is the significance of yellow eyes to a grackle? It turns out that changes in eye color often occur with age. Young grackles start out with brown eyes that become paler with age as a result of hormonal changes. This may indicate the bird's maturity and experience, factors that will help to determine its fitness as a potential mate.

Beginning in late summer, common grackles flock together with starlings and various blackbirds in preparation for the southward migration, the flocks merging into gigantic winter roosts of up to several million birds. There is statistical safety in numbers; an individual in a large flock stands a lesser chance of being taken by a predator than one in a small flock or alone. As with crows, there may also be foraging advantages for young blackbirds, grackles, and starlings who associate with the more experienced birds in the flock.

Common grackles are renowned opportunists. Though they eat mostly insects, fruit, berries, and seeds, in true omnivore fashion they shun little, taking salamanders, frogs, toads, bird eggs, nestlings, crayfish, nestlings, nuts, and even mice.

Red-winged Blackbird

Agelaius phoeniceus

Habitat: marsh, field, grassland
Food: terrestrial invertebrates, seeds
Nest Location: reeds, shrub, 1–8'
Nest Type: cup
Length: 7.25"

For many who are attuned to the natural calendar, robins take a definite back seat to the arrival of male red-winged black-birds as a sure sign of spring. It's not un-usual to see them puff themselves up and let loose with emphatic "konk-la-reeee" calls as they stake their claims over still-frozen marshes or snow-covered meadows.

Researchers have found that the male's flashing red epaulets, which can be covered or exposed at will, are used as a sign of

social status. They also found that territorial males are much more likely to attack intruders whose epaulets are exposed than those who keep them covered. Red-winged males entering an unknown region seeking to establish their own territory or looking for food will keep their epaulets covered to reduce the chances of assault should they wander into another male's territory. Unchallenged, the newcomers will begin to display their red badges. If there is still no response, they may very well proclaim themselves the new owners.

The adaptability of red-winged black-birds that enables them to coexist with yellow-headed blackbirds in the west is evident in the range of habitats they will accept in the east. They favor marshes, but with the destruction of large wetland areas earlier this century, red-wings have established territories and successfully bred in upland grasslands, hayfields, brackish marshes of estuaries, and riverside habitats.

Eastern Meadowlark

Sturnella magna

Habitat: grassland, farm, savanna
Food: terrestrial invertebrates, seeds
Nest Location: ground
Nest Type: cup
Length: 8.5"

Except for the total dissimilarities in their songs, eastern and western meadow-larks are nearly identical in both appearance and behavior. One can often see them in farm country, sitting atop a fencepost and displaying a black "V" against a brilliant yellow breast, or making their labored flight across a meadow, their fanned tail reveal-ing a white border on either side.

Despite its name, the eastern meadow-lark is not a lark at all, but a member of the blackbird family. It is a resident of grass-

lands, and as such eats typical grassland fare, mostly grasshoppers, crickets, beetles, and caterpillars. This species is well adapted for life in a grassland environment, with long legs and a camouflaged back, but most remarkable are their eyes. Placed low toward the base of the bill, they enable the bird to peer under a piece of debris by merely shoving its bill beneath the object and opening the bill to lift, which also posi-tions the mandibles where they can snatch a surprised victim before it has the oppor-tunity to run or hop away.

The nest is a woven cup of grass in a scrape or natural depression at the base of a grass clump, which is woven into an arch-ing roof. So as not to reveal its location, meadowlarks land a distance away from the nest and walk to it through the tall grass. When the altricial nestlings open their mouths to be fed, the colorful red, yellow, orange, and blue lining stimulates the parents' feeding instinct.

Brown-headed Cowbird

Molothrus ater

Habitat: deciduous forest, forest edge, farm, grassland, suburban
Food: terrestrial invertebrates, seeds
Nest Location: parasite
Length: 6.5″

It all started innocently enough. For countless centuries, brown-headed cowbirds were residents of the great plains, following herds of bison and other grazers and eating the insects that were stirred up as they moved along. They needed open spaces in which to feed, and the grasslands were the only extensive areas of the continent not covered by forest. Then came the European settlers, clearing patches of woodland for homesteads and agriculture. Suddenly, the cowbirds were free, able to go wherever they pleased, which they did, to the detriment of songbirds.

You see, brown-headed cowbirds are nest parasites. They lay their eggs in the nests of other birds, usually songbirds smaller than themselves, leaving them to be raised by unwitting foster parents. Most of their victims are not fooled and thwart the cowbird by either destroying its egg(s), building a new nest over the old and laying a new clutch, or abandoning the nest and starting over elsewhere. Still, cowbirds are so successful because the grayish-brown female lays an average of 40 eggs per year in various nests, about 3 per cent of which survive to adulthood. Their eggs hatch sooner than those of most hosts, and the aggressive cowbird chick out-competes its foster siblings for food or shoves them out of the nest.

Northern Oriole

Icterus galbula

Habitat: deciduous and riparian forest, forest edge, suburban, farm
Food: terrestrial invertebrates, fruit, nectar
Nest Location: deciduous tree, 15–30′
Nest Type: basket
Length: 6.5″

The colors of the most beautiful sunset cannot compete with the flaming orange of a male northern oriole. One of the best known song birds in North America both for its brilliance and its unique nest, the northern oriole includes eastern and western races that were once considered separate species, but which were found to interbreed where their ranges met in the Great

Plains. Males of the eastern race have a solid black hood extending to their upper orange breast and black wings with white wingbars, whereas western males have orange cheeks, an orange eye stripe, and large white shoulder patches. Females of both races resemble the males, but is less boldly colored, with muted yellowish-green plumage and less contrast.

The pendulous basket-shaped nest of a northern oriole is both an engineering marvel and a work of art. Suspended from a forked twig near the end of a branch, often directly over water or a road, the sack-like nest looks like a perilous place to deposit their entire productive investment for the year. But orioles are expert weavers, interlacing plant fibers, bark strips, string, yarn, and various other materials so tightly that the nests seldom fall, and often last for more than one season, although they are not reused.

Orioles are insatiable insect eaters, specializing in caterpillars in season, but they also like fruit and plant nectar. They can be lured to your home with orange halves, and oriole nectar feeders are available commercially also.

Western Tanager

Piranga ludoviciana

Habitat: coniferous and mixed forest
Food: terrestrial invertebrates, fruit
Nest Location: conifer, 6–65'
Nest Type: cup
Length: 6.25"

The deep green backdrop of western pine forests where the western tanager spends its summers makes the male's courtship plumage seem even more dazzling by contrast. Female western tanagers are a dull yellowish green so as to be inconspicuous as they incubate eggs in nests built on horizontal forked branches near the tops of tall pines, spruces, and firs. These are largely insect-eaters, consuming mostly bees, wasps, ants, beetles, and caterpillars, but they supplement their diet with fruits and berries. They will visit feeding stations that supply fruit pieces, especially orange slices.

First observed and described to the scientific community by the Lewis and Clark Expedition of 1804–06, this species was undoubtedly better off then than it is today. We like to think of all of the birds we see here as "our" birds, but a great many songbirds that nest in the US and Canada actually spend up to eight months of every year south of Texas. Rampant devastation of tropical habitats fueled by an escalating human population in Central and South America threatens both migratory species, like western tanagers, and non-migratory species alike.

It would be easy to blame our southern neighbors for the alarming drop in migratory songbird populations, except for the glaring fact that the United States is the major market for tropical lumber products and the cheap beef raised on the land after it's cleared. The governments sanctioning the destruction of rainforests are functioning at the subsistence level; if we want to halt these incalculable losses, it is up to us to make it worth their while to stop the destructive cutting and burning.

Scarlet Tanager

Piranga olivacea

Habitat: deciduous forest, mixed forest
Food: terrestrial invertebrates, fruit
Nest Location: deciduous tree, conifer, 20–30'
Nest Type: bowl
Length: 6.25"

At first glance, it seems to be a mirage. The red breeding plumage of male scarlet tanagers is so intense, so mesmerizing, it evokes the same fuzzy impression as looking at a neon light. It's a pity that they hang out so high in the forest canopy where so few people see them, but they are not all that difficult to find if you search for them. They are much more easy-going than the frenzied warblers of the same habitat, so once located, it's fairly easy to keep them in your binoculars' field of view.

Male scarlet tanagers are among the vividly colored birds that undergo a partial "prenuptial" molt. Their winter plumage, which they obtain through a blotchy molt at summer's end, is a greenish-yellow like that of a female, although they retain their black wings. Just prior to breeding season in the spring, the dull feather tips of the male disintegrate and wear off, revealing the luminous ruby hue underneath.

FAMILY FRINGILLIDAE

Northern Cardinal

Cardinalis cardinalis

Habitat: forest edge, thickets, suburban, stream
Food: terrestrial invertebrates, seeds, fruit
Nest Location: shrub, deciduous tree, 1–15′
Nest Type: cup
Length: 7.75″

Because cardinals, especially males with their fire-engine-red head and breast, are common winter residents throughout the eastern United States, their images have come to be popular in this country as Christmas decor. These crested birds abound on cards, on wrapping paper, in ornament shops, with almost anything related to Christmas.

They could very well symbolize fidelity, also, for not only do they form long-term pair bonds (some claim that they mate for life), but by the marked difference be-tween the sexes it is obvious that the pair remains closely associated throughout the year. This is one of the few species of birds in which the song of the buff-colored female rivals the male's in quality. However, whereas the male sings both in courtship and as a means of defining his territory, her song serves mostly to strengthen the pair bond prior to nesting and to communicate with her mate.

Seeds are a primary component of the northern cardinal's diet, as evidenced by their heavy, conical bills which, along with the strong jaw muscles, are supremely adapted for crushing tough seed hulls to liberate the meat inside.

Rose-breasted Grosbeak

Pheucticus ludovicianus

Habitat: deciduous forest, orchard, suburban, thicket
Food: terrestrial invertebrates, fruit, seeds
Nest Location: deciduous tree, shrub, 5–15′
Nest Type: cup
Length: 7.25″

What's black and white and red all over? No, not a newspaper, as the childhood joke goes; it's a male rose-breasted grosbeak! The rosy triangle on his breast shines like a beacon from amidst the young foliage of a sun-dappled springtime forest. Here he belts out a lively robin-like song while drawing the domestic lines of his territory. Unlike colorful males of most other species, the boldly marked male grosbeak takes an active part in nest building and incubation of the clutch, sometimes even singing from the nest. His mate has her own song, another rarity in the bird world. Only a well-hidden nest in the forest understory permits the species to survive with this practice.

Aside from his rosy breast, the male is defined by his black hood, back, and wings, white underparts, and large white wing and rump patches that are most visible in flight. The modest female has a buffy, streaked breast, a brown back, and a white eye stripe. Both sexes are endowed with massive white bills that suggest a diet consisting largely of seeds, but actually they much prefer fruits and insects. The ripening ovaries of fruit tree blossoms are considered a delicacy among rose-breasted grosbeaks.

Evening Grosbeak

Coccothraustes vespertinus

Habitat: coniferous and mixed forest
Food: seeds, fruit, terrestrial invertebrates
Nest Location: conifer, deciduous tree, 20–100′
Nest Type: cup
Length: 7.25″

When a flock of evening grosbeaks descends on your feeders, it becomes evident how they acquired the nick-name "gross-pigs". One can almost hear the squealing of swine around the feeding trough as these beautiful but insatiable birds wolf down sunflower seeds nearly as fast as they can pick them up. A couple of dozen of them can clean out a well stocked feeding station in about an hour and be ready for more as soon as it is refilled.

Male evening grosbeaks are like winged bits of sunshine. The dark brown of their heads blends gradually into a most radiant gold on the breast and back, and a strip of the same slashes each forehead from temple to temple. Large white wing patches are evident both at rest and in flight. The female is a muted gray-brown with tinges of yellow and less distinct wing patches.

They are indeed a mixed blessing at bird feeders, but don't count on seeing them every year. Evening grosbeaks have no migration in the strict sense of the term, but more of a wanderlust. They nest high in the conifers of Canadian and western forests, and when the cone crop is good, they will remain on their breeding grounds, feasting on conifer seeds. When the cone crop is poor, flocks of evening grosbeaks move in a southeasterly direction. There is speculation that large areas of the formerly treeless prairies planted in box elder spurred the wandering of evening grosbeaks by providing a new source of seed. Surely the proliferation of bird feeders in the East keeps them coming back.

Indigo Bunting

Passerina cyanea

Habitat: forest edge, thicket, orchard, farm
Food: terrestrial invertebrates, seeds, fruit
Nest Location: shrub, 1–15′
Nest Type: cup
Length: 4.5″

The plumage of a male indigo bunting is arguably the most intensely blue of any North American bird. As with blue birds, the color of an indigo bunting male is not the result of pigment, but of specialized structures covering each feather barb that bend the light rays passing through them, scattering all but the blue wavelengths. Viewed from certain angles, this feathered sapphire may actually reveal its true colour, dark brown or black. His mate, in contrast, is a small grayish-brown bird with no outstanding features.

Males of this species, whose territories abut one another, recognize their neighbors by voice alone. Each spring, territorial males establish a rigid pecking order determined by brief but decisive clashes. This system keeps physical combat to a minimum, but researchers studying the songs of this species have discovered an interesting twist. It seems that less experienced males learn to imitate their older and usually more dominant neighbors. "Floaters", young or unmated males who have no territory but would like one, recognize the song as that of a superior who earlier kicked their feathered little butt, and steer clear. Thus, the little blue impersonator manages to bluff most challengers, retain both his territory and mate, and breed successfully.

Painted Bunting

Passerina ciris

Habitat: forest edge, thicket, stream, surburban
Food: seeds, terrestrial invertebrates
Nest Location: shrub, deciduous tree, 3–6'
Nest Type: cup
Length: 4.5"

Whoever designed male painted buntings had bizarre tastes. Their colors clash, more so than any other North American bird, yet they are strangely attractive. An American Indian legend has it that as the Great Spirit was creating and coloring birds, he ran short on paints near the end, and so colored the last bird, the painted bunting, with dabs of whatever he had left.

With his blue head, lime-green back, and red breast and rump, a male of this species has no trouble attracting attention, especially that of comparatively dull female painted buntings, undeniably his main objective. She is still rather bright, greenish above and yellowish-green below; no other North American finch is all green.

Most creatures use ritualized displays and bluffs to resolve disputes and live together with a minimum of physical conflict. Such agonistic behavior, as it is called, conserves energy and reduces the risk of injury, clearly beneficial objectives. Not so among painted buntings. Males are known to be quite belligerent, and territorial conflicts often turn into bloody engagements, sometimes ending in the death of one of the combatants. It is hard to imagine the evolutionary advantage of such behavior.

House Finch

Carpodacus mexicanus

Habitat: suburban, urban, farm, thicket, sagebrush, desert
Food: seeds, fruit, buds
Nest Location: deciduous tree, shrub, 5–35', building
Nest Type: cup or cavity
Length: 5.25"

House finches, familiar to most eastern residents as a suburbanite and common visitor to feeders, are relative newcomers in these parts. They are natives of the western United States, where their natural habitat is desert scrub and brushy canyons. In 1941, however, this species was discovered being sold in New York City pet shops as "Hollywood finches", a clear violation of the Migratory Bird Treaty. The resultant outcry from bird enthusiasts prompted at least one store owner to release his house finches, and the race was on. The population stalled on Long Island for several years, but after making their way to the western suburbs of the city, the pace of their invasion quickened. They are now found from Maine through the Great Lake region and south to Florida and the Gulf coast. One source estimates the distance separating the original population and the transplants at less than 100 miles.

House finches are brown birds with streaked breasts. The male's orange-red color is more localized on the brow, breast, and rump than the uniform wine color of the purple finch, which it resembles. They are competing with house sparrows for nest sites and food, and reportedly causing a decline in their population.

Pine Siskin

Carduelis pinus

Habitat: coniferous and mixed woodland, thicket, suburban
Food: seeds, terrestrial invertebrates
Nest Location: conifer, deciduous tree, 8–50′
Nest Type: bowl
Length: 4.25″

Like the evening grosbeak, with whom they share much of their range, pine siskins are more wanderers than migrants, showing up in unpredictable flocks on their winter range. A failure of the seed crop in the boreal forest of Canada results in irruptions of both species, mass invasions of the birds in a southeasterly direction. Pine siskins feed mostly on the seeds of alders, birches, cedars, and hemlocks.

Pine siskins are lively, scrappy little birds, not afraid to stand their ground at the feeder against larger species. They are interesting to watch for this reason alone, if not for their plumage, a mundane brown with profuse streaking on the back and breast. To varying degrees, they show tinges of yellow on their wings and tail, mere hints of the bright yellow exposed in flight. Gregarious pine siskins regularly flock with American goldfinches, their close relatives, in winter. They have a characteristic roller-coaster flight, seen as the flock alternately crowds together and disperses.

American goldfinch

Carduelis tristis

Habitat: field, deciduous and riparian forest, forest edge
Food: seeds, fruit, terrestrial invertebrates
Nest Location: shrub, deciduous tree, 1–30′
Nest Type: cup
Length: 4.25″

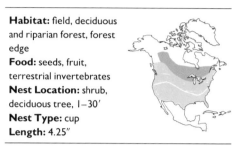

Across the meadows and pastures they fly, and each American goldfinch seems to be riding its own invisible roller coaster. Such an undulating flight pattern is characteristic of birds which are small and fairly weak, and which experience proportionately greater air resistance to forward flight than do larger, stronger birds. To counter this, birds like the goldfinch employ a burst of wingbeats that carries them up and forward, then fold their wings and let their forward momentum carry their streamlined form an additional distance as they begin to drop. Repeated over and over, this flight path becomes a series of evenly spaced hills and valleys.

Males are easily recognized in summer by their lemon-yellow plumage, black cap, and white wingbars on black wings, but in fall they molt to match their olive-drab mates. In spring, a hormonal change triggers the disintegration of their feather tips, gradually exposing the yellow underneath.

American goldfinches are among the latest of North American birds to nest, postponing the start of their families until August or even September. It seems their life cycle is linked to seed-bearing "weeds" of their summer range, especially thistles, a major food source for both adults and nestlings. Unlike many other seed-eaters which feed soft-bodied insects to their new hatchlings, American goldfinches regurgitate seeds that have been shelled and partially digested into the gaping mouths of their brood. They also incorporate the gray, fluffy thistledown into the linings of their tightly woven nest. Due to their reproductive schedule, these goldfinches remain in flocks long after most others have broken up into pairs.

Rufous-sided Towhee

Pipilo erythrophthalmus

Habitat: deciduous forest, forest edge, thickets
Food: terrestrial invertebrates, seeds, fruit
Nest Location: ground, shrub, 0–5'
Nest Type: cup
Length: 7.25"

While enjoying the sights and sounds of United States' forests, many a hiker has been puzzled by loud rustlings that seem to have no origin. Try as they might, many never discover the source of these disembodied stirrings. Not that there's anything supernatural about it; they expect a big noise to come from a big animal, not from the modest rufous-sided towhee. Its habits of nesting on the ground and of thrashing about plant debris on the floor of thickets and deciduous forests in search of insects, seeds, and berries has earned this bird the nickname "ground robin".

These very handsome birds are named partly for the rufous patch on each side and flank. Both sexes show a contrasting white belly and white corners on a dark tail. The jet-black hood and back of the male is brown on females. The irises of most of the adult population's eyes are red, but a white-eyed race manifests itself in the Southeast, and the eyes of juveniles are brown. There is also a western race with white wingbars whose back is spotted with white.

Lark Bunting

Calamospiza melanocorys

Habitat: grassland, field, sagebrush
Food: terrestrial invertebrates, seeds
Nest Location: ground
Nest Type: cup
Length: 6"

Many birds nesting in open terrain, where elevated perches are scarce, advertise their territorial claims with song flights instead of singing from a prominent perch. Male lark buntings are only weakly territorial, and while they perform territorial song flights, ascending rapidly and then floating in butterfly fashion on stiffened wings over their domain, it is more important to courtship than anything else. It is not uncommon to see many males pursuing overlapping courses in half-hearted territorial displays with little conflict between them. They are equally tolerant of each other when nesting, often grouped in a loose colony and even foraging in flocks.

Except for their flashing white wing patches, males are jet-black. Females are more sparrowlike in appearance, brown with coarse black streaks, and showing much white in their wings. The large, conical bill is decidedly un-sparrowlike, however. They are fond of all types of seeds and grain, as well as many insects, particularly grasshoppers. They are seen as a good omen by some farmers, who believe that lark buntings arrive in abundance in anticipation of a bumper crop.

Lark Sparrow

Chondestes grammacus

Habitat: field, thicket, grassland, savanna
Food: seeds, terrestrial invertebrates
Nest Location: ground, shrub, 0–7'
Nest Type: cup
Length: 5.75"

If your children were threatened, would you stand and fight or run away? Nearly all of us would unhesitatingly defend our offspring, yet the lark sparrow is one of many birds whose parental instincts tell them to flee, but not without great fanfare. These tactics, called distraction displays, are employed when an intruder ventures too close to the nest or fledglings. By conspicuously exposing itself with a feigned injury or illness, the parent diverts a predator's attention with the promise of an easy meal. Spreading her tail and fluttering one or both wings in an unnatural posture, the lark sparrow labors away from her enemy, but always manages to stay just a step or two ahead. After she has led her pursuer a sufficient distance away, she is suddenly cured and flies off, leaving her confused and hungry follower behind.

A lark sparrow's head is handsomely marked with a distinctive pattern of chestnut, black, and white. This, combined with white corners on a black tail and a central spot on its unstreaked gray breast, makes it one of the more easily recognized sparrows. The male is noted for his flamboyant courtship dance.

Dark-eyed Junco

Junco hyemalis

Habitat: coniferous and mixed forest, forest edge, thicket, suburban
Food: seeds, terrestrial invertebrates
Nest Location: ground
Nest Type: cup
Length: 5.25″

The different races of dark-eyed junco were, until recently, considered to be four separate species. Upon investigation, however, it was found that they hybridized freely wherever their ranges overlapped. Only one race, formerly the slate-colored junco, is found across North America, and they are mostly restricted to the boreal forest and the Appalachians during the summer. The Oregon, white-winged, gray-headed, and Guadalupe races occupy various ranges in western North America. All races of the dark-eyed junco are small ground-feeders that flash white outer tail feathers in flight and have conical pink bills.

Juncos, with the flash pattern they show in flight, symbolize the puzzle of the many birds that deliberately draw attention to themselves as they flee danger. One would think that this would put them at an evolutionary disadvantage and that the genes for such a trait would have been weeded out of the population long ago. Flash patterns often serve a cohesive function, keeping the group together instead of scattering. In attempting to flee alone, a bird invites a one-on-one chase with an enemy built for pursuit. Birds that have evolved a cohesive signal, like the junco's flash pattern, and surround themselves with, say, 19 other juncos, reduce their odds of becoming a victim to 1 in 20, assuming an unrealistic 100 per cent success rate on the part of the predator.

Chipping Sparrow

Spizella passerina

Habitat: coniferous and mixed forest, forest edge, farm, orchard, suburban
Food: terrestrial invertebrates, seeds
Nest Location: conifer, deciduous tree, 1–11′
Nest Type: cup
Length: 4.75″

This little sparrow, undistinguished in the flesh except for its rapidly trilling song, a rusty cap outlined in white and black, and an unstreaked gray breast, is most noted for the female's choice of building materials for her nest. Chipping sparrows incorporate so much hair in building their nests that they acquired the name "hair bird" from our forebearers.

"Chippies", as they are affectionately called by some, were in their heyday during the settlement of North America, when horses and other beasts of burden were a regular part of the landscape. To this day, chipping sparrows can be seen in the spring tugging at the manes or tails of horses in spring pastures and making off with a few prized strands. Where horses are scarce, they build their nests with grasses and rootlets, still preferring to line them with hair from animals if possible.

Nests are so important in the life cycles of most birds, serving as a cradle for the eggs, a crib for the nestlings, and a playpen for those larger species who mature slowly, that we would be amiss not to study them as well as their builders. Nesting is a very demanding time, so do wait until the birds have finished with their nests for the year before examining them closely, and remember that it is illegal to possess bird nests without special, hard-to-get permits.

White-throated Sparrow

Zonotrichia albicollis

Habitat: coniferous woodland, mixed woodland, forest edge, thicket
Food: terrestrial invertebrates, seeds, fruit
Nest: ground, shrub, 0–3'
Length: 5.75"

While the white-throated sparrow is neither the most common nor most widespread sparrow in North America, its clear, slightly quavering song is surely one of the most well-known, second perhaps only to that of the ubiquitous song sparrow. This bird nests primarily in the boreal forest, that great expanse of spruces and fir that stretches from coast to coast and across Canada and from northern New England and the Great Lake region to the Arctic tundra. Males will sing half-heartedly throughout the winter, but begin in earnest about March, long before they've left their

winter range across the southeastern half of the United States. At this point, the song must be strictly a courtship ploy, since the breeding territory to which they faithfully return is still far away.

White-throated sparrows are ground-feeders easily lured to feeding stations by scattering seed directly on the ground. Except for their white throat, lemon-yellow

spots in front of their eyes, and darker bill, this species could easily be mistaken for the white-crowned sparrow, a more western and northern species that shares the same winter range. Both display a boldly black-and-white striped crown (white-throats also occur with buff instead of white stripes), but the bill of a white-crowned sparrow is distinctly pink.

Song Sparrow

Melospiza melodia

Habitat: thicket, marsh, forest edge, riparian forest, suburban, farm
Food: terrestrial invertebrates, seeds
Nest Location: ground, shrub, 0–3'
Nest Type: cup
Length: 5.5"

The virtuoso among sparrows, the male song sparrow is reported to have a repertoire of roughly 1,000 variations on up to 20 different tunes. Females also sing during courtship, but not with the gusto of males. Singing ability is the prime attribute of this otherwise drab bird, to which its translated Latin name, "song-finch with a pleasing

song", attests. Its other field marks include a pale breast with diffuse but dark streaks and a large central breast spot.

While there are exceptions, the basic rule seems to be that calls are mostly in-nate, or instinctive, but songs must be learned for the most part. Birds are apparently born with a genetic model of what their songs should sound like, and develop them by matching the sounds they hear from adults with the model in their brains. Juveniles begin with a vague subsong which bears little resemblance to songs of adults, but apparently provides the young birds with building blocks to play with as they work the sounds into a "plastic" song, variable but closer to the finished product, while filtering out the sounds that do not fit the model. The final "crystallized" songs of an adult's repertoire contain far fewer sounds than does the original subsong.

This process has been demonstrated with hatchlings reared in isolated soundproofed chambers. With no opportunity to hear adult songs, the birds could not reproduce them, and the jumbled songs they produced were not recognized by others of their own species.

Glossary

Aquatic – a life cycle closely linked to water.
Barb – parallel hair-like structures composing the vane of flight and contour feathers.
Barbule – one of many miniscule appendages extending from the barbs of feathers.
Birding – bird watching.
Brood – the group of offspring hatched from one clutch of egss.
Call – a short vocal communication, shorter than a song.
Carrion – prey found dead.
Cavity – a chamber, usually inside a tree or a stump.
Clutch – a cluster of eggs in a nest, all laid before any have hatched.
Colonial – birds that build nests and rear offspring in close proximity to one another.
Coniferous – a reference to trees bearing seeds in cones.
Courtship – ritualized behaviour intended to attract a mate.
Deciduous – a reference to trees that drop all of their leaves for part of the year.
Display – ritualized vocal or visual behaviour conveying a specific message.
Field mark – any distinguishing feature.
Fledgling – a young bird that has left the nest but is still dependent upon its parents for at least some of its food.
Hierarchy – A social "pecking order" that minimizes physical conflict and conserves time and energy.
Incubation – the act of maintaining eggs at the proper temperature, usually via body heat.

Invertebrate – animals without backbones.
Lek – ancestral breeding grounds where males of certain grassland species gather to perform courtship displays.
Mandibles – the two parts of a birds bill analogues to jaws.
Molt – the process of shedding and replacing feathers.
Monogamy – an exclusive mating of one male with one female.
Migration – the seasonal movement of a species from one region or climate to another.
Nest – the place where eggs are laid, may or may not consist of an actual physical structure created by the bird.
Nestling – a young bird still in the nest, totally dependent upon its parents for food.
Omnivore – an animal whose diet includes large portions of both plants and animals in many forms.
Pair bond – the emotional link that keeps a monogamous pair together for a given period of time.
Plumage – a collective reference to feathers.
Polyandry – a system in which one female mates with more than one male during the breeding season.

Polygyny – a system in which one male mates with more than one female during the breeding season.
Primaries – the outermost and longest flight feathers on a bird's wing.
Preening – the act of feather maintenance using bills or claws.
Race – a consistent variation within a species; a subspecies.
Range – the normal geographic limits of an organism's distribution.
Raptor – a bird of prey characterized by strong, curved talons, a hooked bill, and excellent binocular vision.
Riparian – associated with rivers or streams.
Roost – the place where a bird sleeps or the act of sleeping.
Shorebird – generally, wading birds that feed while standing in shallow water, on mud flats, or near the water's edge.
Snag – a standing dead tree.
Song – vocal communication, longer and more elaborate than a call.
Species – a group of organisms capable of interbreeding to producing fertile offspring.
Terrestial – life cycles spent mostly out of water.
Territory – any area defended for the purposes of nesting, mating, or feeding.
Vane – the flattened portion of flight and contour feathers composed of parallel barbs extending from the main shaft.
Waterfowl – a collective reference to ducks, geese, swans, and mergansers.

Bibliography

Bull, John and John Farrand Jr. 1977. *The Audubon Society Field Guide to North American Birds, Eastern Region*. New York, NY. Alfred A Knopf, Inc.

Cassidy, James (Project Editor). 1990. *Book of North American Birds*. Pleasantville, NY. Reader's Digest Association, Inc.

Cruickshank, Allan D. and Helen G. Cruickshank. 1958. *1,001 Questions Answered About Birds*. New York, NY. Dover Publications, Inc.

Dennis, John V. 1975. *A Complete Guide to Bird Feeding*. New York, NY. Alfred A. Knopf, Inc.

Ehrlich, Paul R., David S. Dobkin, and Darryl Wheye. 1988. *The Birder's Handbook: A Field Guide to the Natural History of North American Birds*. New York, NY. Simon & Schuster, Inc.

Gooders, John. 1990. *The Practical Ornithologist*. New York, NY. Simon & Schuster, Inc.

Harrison, George H. 1979. *The Backyard Bird Watcher*. New York NY. Simon & Schuster, Inc.

Kress, Stephen W. 1985. *The Audubon Society Guide to Attracting Birds*. New York, NY. Charles Scribner's Sons.

Peterson, Roger Tory. 1980. *A Field Guide to the Birds East of the Rockies*. Boston, MA. Houghton Mifflin Co.

Proctor, Dr. Noble. 1985. *Garden Birds*. Emmaus, PA. Rodale Press, Inc.

Proctor, Dr. Noble. 1988. *Song Birds*. Emmaus, PA. Rodale Press, Inc.

Reilly, Edgar M., and Gorton Carruth. 1987. *The Bird Watcher's Diary*. New York, NY. Harper & Row, Publishers, Inc.

Robbins, Chandler S., Bertel Bruun, and Herbert S. Zim. 1966.
Birds of North America. New York, NY. Golden Press.

Stokes, Donald W. 1979. *A Guide to Bird Behavior, Volume I*. Boston, MA. Little, Brown, & Co.

Stokes, Donald W. and Lillian Q. Stokes. 1983. *A Guide to Bird Behavior, Volume II*. Boston MA. Little, Brown, & Co.

Stokes, Donald W. and Lillian Q. Stokes. 1989. *A Guide to Bird Behavior, Volume III*. Boston MA. Little, Brown, & Co.

Weidensaul, Scott. 1989. *Garden Birds of North America*. New York, NY. W.H. Smith Publishers, Inc.

Welty, Joel Carl. 1975. *The Life of Birds*. Philadelphia, PA. W.B. Saunders Company.

For Further Information, Contact

American Birding Association
P.O. Box 4335
Austin, TX 78765

American Ornithologist's Union, Inc.
National Museum of Natural History
Smithsonian Institution
Washington, D.C. 20560

Canadian Nature Federation
453 Sussex Dr.
Ottawa, Canada K1N 6Z4

Canadian Wildlife Federation
1673 Carling Ave.
Ottawa, Ontario K2A 32L

Cooper Ornithological Society
Dept. of Biology
University of California
Los Angeles, CA 90024

Cornell Laboratory of Ornithology
159 Sapsucker Woods Road
Ithaca, NY 14850

National Audubon Society
950 Third Avenue
New York, NY 10022

National Wildlife Federation
1400 16th St., NW
Washington, D.C. 20036

Wilson Ornithological Society
c/o Josselyn Van Tyne Memorial Library
Museum of Zoology
University of Michigan
Ann Arbor, MI 48104

Index